HE STILL SPEAKS

ABOUT THE TOLER BROTHERS

The Toler Brothers have a combined 75 years of ministry experience. They include Stan, a best-selling author, speaker, and pastor of Trinity Church of the Nazarene in Oklahoma City; Terry, a platinum-selling songwriter, speaker, and vice president of Southern Nazarene University in Bethany, Oklahoma; and Mark, a humorist, speaker, and pastor of First Church of the Nazarene in Edmond, Oklahoma. With gifted abilities, a contagious sense of humor, and a compassionate spirit born out of childhood tragedies, the Tolers have been featured in TV appearances, concerts, seminars, and conventions internationally.

For More Information
The Toler Brothers
P.O. Box 892170
Oklahoma City, OK 73189
www.TolerBrothersTrio.com

HE STILL SPEAKS

The
Toler
Brothers

BEACON HILL PRESS
OF KANSAS CITY

Library of Congress Cataloging-in-Publication Data

Toler, Stan.
   He still speaks / Stan Toler, Terry Toler, Mark Toler-Hollingsworth.
      p. cm.
   Includes bibliographical references.
   ISBN 978-0-8341-2384-7 (pbk.)
   1. Christian Life. I. Toler, Terry Nelson. II. Toler-Hollingsworth, Mark. III. Title.

   BV4501.3.T625 2008
   242—dc22

                                                                    2008006469

10 9 8 7 6 5 4 3 2 1

This book is dedicated to the memory
of our dad, William Aaron Toler, and to our mom, Loretta.

We also offer special recognition to our stepfather,
Jack Hollingsworth, who has been "Dad" to us for
over forty years. Thanks for loving us and for
making sure we had plenty to eat and a good
college education. You are our superhero!

CONTENTS

FOREWORD

If anyone should write a book of humorous and inspiring stories, it's the Tolers. In all the years I've been around them, I've never known them to be without a story. Whether it's told during a concert, a message, or over a cup of coffee, Stan, Terry, and Mark can add a quote, a joke, or an illustration that will make your day.

But their lives aren't just about good old West Virginia storytelling. I've also known them to be men of great faith. They are survivors of some tragic circumstances, yet they still wear that Toler smile. They don't live in the past; they live for the future. And everyone around them can feel their sense of hope.

I have watched them in their ministries. I have read their books and sung their songs. They're for real. And they have a unique way of making you believe in yourself—and believe in their Lord.

I count it a privilege to recommend this book to anyone who needs to be inspired and encouraged. These songs and stories will make you laugh and cry. But you won't be what you once were after reading and applying the principles in these writings.

Each chapter reveals the Toler's signature personalities. It's their style of writing. It's their mission of pointing people to Jesus. It's their heart for the hurting. It's all there. And it's all Toler. Best thing about the Toler brothers is that they live what they sing and preach. You will love this book.

W. Talmadge Johnson
General Superintendent Emeritus
Church of the Nazarene

PREFACE

Every song has a story. Some stories are known only to the writers and their closest friends. When revealed, the story gives the song an even deeper meaning for the singer, listener, or reader.

And as you know, every one of your stories has a song—a melody or lyric that soothed your soul during the storm, that gave you a point of emotional reference and guided your spirit to a place of acceptance and peace.

He Still Speaks is an amazing journal of the lives and triumphs of three brothers who are gifted not only with musical talent but also with the ability to express their faith, foibles, and fortunes in writing in a way that makes people laugh out loud—then pause and reflect with thanksgiving and renewed faith.

Raised in one of the poorest counties in America, the Toler Brothers didn't even have a radio in their home. Their entertainment was singing around an old upright piano in the living room of their West Virginia home. The Southern gospel harmonies born from that humble time have provided the soundtrack for a combined seventy-five years of worldwide ministries that have touched literally millions of lives.

Stan Toler is a best-selling author, successful pastor, and international seminar leader. Terry Toler is a three-time Grammy contributor and platinum-selling songwriter as well as vice president of a Christian university. Mark Toler-Hollignsworth is a well known humorist, speaker, and pastor. In this book these brothers blend their gifted voices with the experiences that helped them rise above childhood adversities, including the tragic death of their father and the destruction of their home by fire.

You may have heard their songs; now read their stories—stories that reflect their unique talents and their common touch, stories as homespun as a braided rug and as graceful as a spring meadow, stories of grace and grit and sometimes good old Southern grits. These are funny stories, faithful stories, human stories.

The brothers get together as often as their busy schedules allow. Sometimes they meet for lunch and a laugh, sometimes to strategize the objectives of their ministries and critique their performance, and sometimes they just get together at Stan's house for a haircut. Stan is not only the barber in the family; he's also the elder brother who kept the family together after the sudden loss of their father.

Terry is the songwriter in the family. Whether in a solo effort like "Thinkin' About Home" or a cowriting project like "You Can Depend on Jesus," Terry has the ability to bare his soul on manuscript paper and craft melodies of his faith in a way that makes others want to know his Savior. From Grammy winners to weekend warriors, many Southern gospel groups have recorded his simple songs of God's favor and performed them on the stages of sold-out auditoriums and the platforms of country churches across America. His experiences as a musician, pastor, and administrator give him a godly insight into the trials of twenty-first-century life.

Mark, living under the eagle eyes of the elder brothers, has emerged as a Christian leader in his own right without losing his touch for the humorous side of life. Whether in a hilarious stand-up routine or in a stirring gospel message, he knows how to get the point across without pointing fingers. He has no trouble holding his own with his platinum-winning songwriter best-selling author brothers. His writing reflects his earthy observations, and his gift for blending the bread of life with the butter of living makes you hungry for more.

He Still Speaks is more than a book or song title; it is a belief that God's Holy Spirit is leading the church to its Homecoming Day. Sure, it will have to maneuver around some potholes and construction zones. Sure it will have to do combat with the forces of hell. But as you will see in this book, there isn't an obstacle that's taller than the Christ. And there isn't a valley so wide that it will not echo with the song of salvation.

> The still small voice of God is heard
> Above the doubters of this world;
> His timeless word rings out with hope today.
> He still speaks, I know His voice.

Jerry Brecheisen

ACKNOWLEDGEMENTS

The Toler Brothers offer special thanks to Jerry Brecheisen, Lawrence W. Wilson, Lyn Rayn, Michael Sykes, Bonnie Perry, Barry Russell, and the whole Beacon Hill Team.

We also wish to thank our family members for their enduring love and encouragement to do ministry through sermon and song.

STAN, TERRY, AND MARK

Shout praises to the Lord!
Everyone who serves Him,
come and praise His name.
Let the name of the Lord
be praised, both now and forevermore.
From dawn until sunset
the name of the Lord
deserves to be praised.

—PSALM 113:1–3 (CEV)

Praise is the antidote for a tired spirit.
—TERRY TOLER

1

STARTING NOW

Mark Toler-Hollingsworth

STARTING NOW

By Terry Toler and Michael Sykes

Chorus

Starting now let your praise begin,
Starting now why don't you join right in;
Don't wait a minute longer,
To lift holy praise to Him;
Starting now—let your praise begin

We're invited by the Father,
We gather in Jesus name,
The power of the Spirit's in this place;
Everyone who has breath is called to enter in,
Starting now—let your praise begin.

For the tired, praise is the answer,
To the sick, a healing stream;
For the helpless there's a reason,
To lift up your voice and sing;
Everyone who has breath is called to enter in,
Starting now—let your praise begin.

Bridge

Sing hallelujah—glory hallelujah—hallelujah to His name;

Sing hallelujah—glory hallelujah—hallelujah to His name;

Sing hallelujah—glory hallelujah—hallelujah to His name.

Chorus

Starting now let your praise begin,

Starting now why don't you join right in;

Don't wait a minute longer,

To lift holy praise to Him,

Starting now—let you praise begin.[1]

TIME TO PRAISE

Praise is a verb. It means to express approval or admiration, to commend, extol, or glorify. Praise—everyone can do it, and now is the time to begin. There's no need to wait until Sunday, do it now!

"Oh, but I'm so tired." Praise will give you energy!

"Oh, but I'm so sick, I just don't feel like it." Praise has been scientifically proven to have healing antibodies.

"Well, I can't think of anything to praise the Lord for." That's okay, the Bible gives you a list of three things for which you can praise:

Praise God for *past* blessings. Isaiah 25:1 says, "LORD, you are my God. I honor you and praise you, because you have done amazing things. You have always done what you said you would do; you have done what you planned long ago" (NCV).

Praise God for *present* blessings. Psalm 103:1–5 declares, "With all my heart I praise the LORD, and with all that I am I praise His holy name! The LORD forgives our sins, heals us when we are sick, and protects us from death. His kindness and love are a crown on our heads. Each day that we live, He provides for our needs and gives us the strength of a young eagle" (CEV).

Praise God for *potential* blessings. Joel 2:21 records, "be glad and rejoice: for the LORD will do great things" (KJV).

Why don't you just stand up right now and shout, "Hallelujah! Glory hallelujah! Hallelujah to His name!" It'll make you feel better, and God will get a kick out of it too!

NO WRONG WAY TO PRAISE

The Bible talks a great deal about the use of hands when we praise the Lord. For example: when we praise Him, we are to clap our hands. Psalm 47:1 says, "All of you nations, clap your hands and shout joyful praises to God (CEV). The Bible also says that when we bring our praise to God, we're to lift our hands. Psalm 134:2 says, "Lift up your hands in the sanctuary and praise the LORD."

Now I don't mean to brag, but you can blindfold me, take me into any church in America (preferably one in Florida or Hawaii), remove the blindfold once I am in the sanctuary, and I can tell you what denomination that church is, simply by watching the congregation praise the Lord. It's all in the hands.

For example, my church, The Church of the Nazarene, is a "one-hander" church. That is, when we praise the Lord and get blessed about all He has done for us, we praise Him by lifting one hand. It usually starts at about half-staff, but when we really get fired up, that ol' Nazarene hand can shoot twelve o'clock straight up!

Mark

The Pentecostals are "two-handers." Yes sir, when a Pentecostal gets blessed there's no messin' around—it's two hands in the air with no reservations whatsoever! I like the way Pentecostals praise the Lord; they are such happy people. The Church of the Nazarene was initially named The Pentecostal Church of the Nazarene, but we later dropped the Pentecostal part. I guess we decided we just weren't all that happy!

There are lots of other examples. My Presbyterian friends tell me that they sit on their hands during the praise part of worship for fear they might get carried away. And I know of some other Christian folk who won't even shake hands in church!

Some people say there's a praise and worship war going on in the church today. Some like to project praise choruses onto the wall and sing them multiple times accompanied by loud instruments such as electric guitars and drums. Some others won't praise the Lord at all unless there's a hymnal in their hand and an organ and piano playing (upright preferred)—although usually singing the first and last verse is sufficient.

Here's what I believe: God loves all of it—electric or acoustic, loud or soft, instruments or no instruments. He created us for praise. In Isaiah 43:21, God spoke of "the people I formed for myself that they may proclaim my praise."

Tolers on their way to church

Talking about singing out of the hymnal or from slides projected on the wall makes me think of the time my brothers saved my life during a revival meeting. When we were little boys, we each got our share of spankings for talking in church. Lots of folks ask us how it is that all three of us ended up being preachers. It's really pretty simple: we got spanked so much for talking in church that we figured we might as well get paid for it!

Mom and Dad could put a pretty good whoopin' on us. In church, however, Mom couldn't get to us because she was the church pianist. So when Mom was playing the piano and we acted up, she would snap her fingers and stare us down with a look that would make a mountain lion tremble in its tracks.

Mom also used the option of taking us downstairs after the offertory. Trust me, you didn't want to have to go downstairs. Mom whipped us so hard *our* kids are dizzy! I'm convinced there wouldn't be any juvenile crime in America if we could just load Mom up in the car and let her do some "drive-by whoopin's!"

Dad, on the other hand was a "thumper." He had working man's hands; hands the size of ham hocks. He would line us up in the pew in front of him so he could keep an eye on us at all times. If we acted up, he would thump us in the back of the head. In contrast, I don't understand the way kids are disciplined these days. When a kid gets in trouble these days, he gets a *timeout*. We didn't get timeouts—we got *blackouts*! Daddy would thump us in the back of the head so hard we would see stars. One Tuesday night during a revival meeting, the evangelist got a little long winded. Brother Stanley was stretched out in the pew sawing logs and mumbling in his sleep, "Pharaoh, let my people go." Brother Terry and I passed the time by amusing ourselves with a rather competitive game of Hangman on the back of a tithe envelope. Well, as older brothers sometimes do, Terry started cheating, and I wasn't about to have it. I threw my pencil to the floor, wadded up the tithe envelope, rolled up my shirt sleeves, and was about to go Old Testament on Terry. Suddenly I felt Daddy's middle finger imbedded in the back of my head.

I saw stars, I heard angels singing, I saw a bright light and started walking towards it. I saw Granny, I saw my pet parakeet Peetey who had passed away while I was at children's camp, and I saw Uncle Chub—that was quite a surprise; he must have thrown up a Hail Mary there at the end. Before I knew what was happening, I was blacked out on the hardwood floor of the Fifth Avenue church. When I came to, my brothers were standing over me, fanning me with hymnals and asking me how many fingers they were holding up. They saved my life! Years later, however, this thought occurred to me: What if we had attended a church that sang praise choruses projected on the sanctuary wall? There wouldn't have been a single hymnal for my brothers to fan me with. I might have died!

VICTORY IN PRAISE

One of my favorite Old Testament passages is found in 2 Chronicles. It records a time when God's people were being attacked by a host of armies. The Moabites, Ammonites, and Meunites joined forces to make war on King Jehoshaphat and the people Judah. They had so many armies joined together that I think they even had some *Termites* and *Gesundheits*, maybe even a few *Stalagtites* thrown in there! So King Jehoshaphat, after much prayer and fasting, gave this battle plan to his army: "After consulting with the people, the king ordered some musicians to put on the robes they wore on sacred occasions and to march ahead of the army, singing: "Praise the Lord! His love is eternal!" (2 Chronicles 20:21 GNB).

Do you get the picture? A vast army from three different tribes were about to attack, and King Jehoshaphat said, "I want the choir to robe up and sing some praise choruses." Now after twenty-seven years of ministry and a total of forty-eight years in the church, I confess that I've heard some pretty bad choirs. There are some church choirs that ought to sing "On a hill far away"—literally. Some choirs would do a better job singing on the front lines of the battlefield than they would behind the modesty panel. Why on earth would King Jehoshaphat do dat? (I'm sorry; sometimes I just can't help it). He had the choir march ahead of the army, singing praises to the Lord, because the Lord inhabits the praises of His people. When you are being attacked, perhaps the best thing for you to do is to sing a song of praise. Psalm 150 is a good song to sing:

Praise the LORD.
> Praise God in his sanctuary;
> praise Him in his mighty heavens.
Praise Him for his acts of power;
> praise Him for his surpassing greatness.
Praise Him with the sounding of the trumpet,
> praise Him with the harp and lyre,
praise Him with tambourine and dancing,
> praise Him with the strings and flute,
praise Him with the clash of cymbals,
> praise Him with resounding cymbals.
Let everything that has breath praise the LORD.
> Praise the LORD.

Here is the rest of the story: After the choir began to sing praise to the Lord, the Bible says in Second Chronicles 20:22–26 (GNB):

When they began to sing, the Lord threw the invading armies into a panic. The Ammonites and the Moabites attacked the Edomite army and completely destroyed it, and then they turned on each other in savage fighting. When the Judean army reached a tower that was in the desert, they looked towards the enemy and saw that they were all lying on the ground, dead. Not one had escaped. Jehoshaphat and his troops moved in to take the loot, and they found many cattle, supplies, clothing, and other valuable objects. They spent three days gathering the loot, but there was so much that they could not take everything. On the fourth day they assembled in the Valley of Beracah and praised the Lord for all he had done. That is why the valley is called "Beracah."

If you're in a battle, praise is the answer. Terry's song says if you're tired, praise is the answer! If you're sick, praise is the answer! If you're helpless, praise is the answer!" Our pastor at the Fifth Avenue Church, Rev. C. O. Waters, used to say, "When you can't pray your way through, praise your way through!" Now is the time to let your praise begin!

*J*esus reached out his hand and
touched the man. "I am willing," he said.
"Be clean!" And immediately the
leprosy left him.

—LUKE 5:13

When we reach out to touch, we are not doing the touching.
It's Jesus doing the touching. He touches through our lives.

—Source Unknown

2

HE TOUCHED ME

Stan Toler

HE TOUCHED ME

By William J. Gaither

Shackled by a heavy burden,
'Neath a load of guilt and shame—
Then the hand of Jesus touched me,
And now I am no longer the same.

Chorus
He touched me, Oh He touched me,
And oh the joy that floods my soul!
Something happened, and now I know,
He touched me and made me whole.

Since I met this blessed Savior,
Since He cleansed and made me whole,
I will never cease to praise Him—
I'll shout it while eternity rolls.

Chorus
He touched me, Oh He touched me,
And oh the joy that floods my soul!
Something happened, and now I know,
He touched me and made me whole.[2]

A Special Song

Songwriter Bill Gaither said he gave his life to Christ behind the auditorium of a 4-H park in Ohio when he was nineteen years old. He had just finished singing a concert with his brother and sister in the auditorium, but he wasn't happy with the direction of his life.[3] Jesus touched Gaither's life that day, and the gospel music world would be forever changed as a result. In 2000 the American Society of Composers and Performers named Bill and his wife, Gloria, Gospel Songwriters of the Century. Their classic gospel song "He Touched Me"—one of the many that have blessed people around the world—is one of the most popular songs in the history of religious music.

Stan

The song has special meaning for the Toler Brothers. It was the first song we sang together in church. We had been rehearsing since we were strong enough to carry a tune around the house. But the moment of that first performance stands out in my memory. The three of us stood on the small platform of the historic Fifth Avenue Church in Columbus, Ohio. With the preacher in his pulpit chair, the large wooden pulpit, and some flowers left over from a wedding that week, there was hardly room enough for us on the platform—let alone for the butterflies that were doing jumping jacks in our stomachs! Sound systems were a bit different back then, so we weren't sure if the dear brother with a hearing problem who always sat on the back pew would be able to hear one word of the song. If I remember right, we would have been stretching to push twenty-five watts out of that Bogen amplifier. And the microphone had probably been bought at a scratch-and-dent sale at Sears. Besides that, it was difficult to get a through a song in those days without hearing "Ten-four, good buddy" picked up from a passerby with a citizens band radio.

I don't know if we got the harmony right or remembered all the lyrics that day (Terry would remember! I think he has the price and purchase dates for all of his socks filed on a computer somewhere); I just know it was a special moment in our lives. Our dad, who died in a construction accident when we were young, loved to sing gospel music. His music carried beyond the four walls of our home or our church—it carried into our hearts. He birthed a song in us that has not faded over the many years since he sang his last note on earth or his first note in heaven.

He Touched Me

"He Touched Me" is a special song for another reason. I was fourteen, and had just returned from youth camp. To some, youth camp was like a temporary sentence in a reformatory, but to me it was a holiday. At youth camp, I had my own bed. And youth camp wasn't just about pillow fights in the dormitory that had walls reaching only halfway to the ceiling. It wasn't just about food fights in the cement block cafeteria, s'mores around the campfire, or meeting girls from other churches in the district for "walking dates" around the campground. Youth camp was a place where eternal choices were made at a rough wooden altar at the front of the well-worn tabernacle. It was a place where I made some of the most important decisions of my life, including answering God's call to be a preacher of the gospel.

When I got home from camp, weary from sleepless nights, and tired of macaroni-and-cheese recipes, I told my mom about that decision. As usual, she affirmed God's call on my life and smiled at the memory of holding me in her arms during an infant dedication ceremony at the church. Mom's love for the Lord was a lighthouse in our lives—always there, always lit, and always giving us safe direction.

Yet I knew there were others who needed to know about my decision—especially those dear people at Fifth Avenue Church. They had made a commitment to the Toler family that would not soon be forgotten. Their love and generosity had often kept our little financial boat afloat when the storms came at us. I knew I'd have to find just the right time to tell them about the direction God had given for my life.

It happened on the Sunday I was asked to sing during the evening service. I chose "He Touched Me." I chose the song for two reasons. First, it was a song that was in my voice range at the time, which, during those teenage years, was changing direction faster than a gnat in a hurricane. Second, it was my testimony song.

I began the song as usual, singing, "Shackled by a heavy burden, 'neath the load of sin and shame, then the hand of Jesus touched me, and now I am no longer the same." But after the chorus, I stopped. Something was stirring in my young heart. The Holy Spirit gave me a big ol' nudge, and I had to tell the people. I don't remember the exact words, but I remember blurting out that God had called me to preach. In those days, folks weren't quiet about God being in the room! It wasn't uncommon for some of them to have a "shoutin' spell" now and then, and they sure had one that day. "Hallelujah!" and "Amen!" ricocheted off the ceiling. Revival had broken out, and nobody was in a hurry to look for a fire extinguisher.

Someone in the audience started a song—I guess they forgot I was supposed to be singing "He Touched Me"—and everyone joined in. Then they sang another, and another, until the service turned into a concert of praise. Daddy must have heard it in heaven, and he probably joined in! Eventually folks settled down long enough for our pastor, Rev. C. O. Waters, to preach. He was about to give the benediction when someone interrupted him. "Pastor!" he said, "Stanley hasn't finished his song." Thank the Lord, someone had remembered.

Pastor Waters called me back to the platform and asked me to sing another verse. I sang, "Since I met this blessed Savior, since He cleansed and made me whole, I will never cease to praise Him, I'll shout it while eternity rolls." Some of the saints couldn't wait for eternity to roll! Shouts of praise started all over again and we "had church" until just about midnight. Just before he dismissed the crowd, the pastor gave a surprise announcement. He said, "Stanley will be preaching next Sunday night." I didn't know if I'd be ready to preach my first sermon in just one week, but I did know that Jesus had touched my life and that I would never be the same.

Last Easter Sunday with Daddy in 1962

THE TOUCH OF JESUS

The account of Jesus healing of the leper shows us what a difference His touch makes, "While Jesus was in one of the towns, a man came along who was covered with leprosy. When he saw Jesus, he fell with his face to the ground and begged him, 'Lord, if you are willing, you can make me clean.' Jesus reached out his hand and touched the man. 'I am willing,' he said. 'Be clean!' And immediately the leprosy left him" (Luke 5:12–13).

THE TOUCH OF AFFECTION

"I am willing," Jesus said. His heart was full of love for the diseased man. Others had gone out of their way to pass him by, but not Jesus. He went out of His way to help him. Bitterness and emptiness had been the man's life. He sat by the road and watched the world go by, alone and lonely. He needed the touch of healing. Not just for his body, but also for his soul. Jesus touched both.

In the same way, Jesus is reaching out to you. He wants to touch you with His grace and power. No matter where you've been, no matter what you've done, and no matter what has happened, He loves you. Others may pass you by, Jesus will stop by. Others may ostracize you, Jesus will include you. His is a willing heart, a heart that wants you to be whole—to be holy. But what you can't achieve for yourself, Jesus has already done for you. He accomplished our salvation on the cross of Calvary. "If we confess our sins, he is faithful and just and will forgive us our sins and purify us from all unrighteousness" (1 John. 1:9).

THE TOUCH OF LIBERATION

"Be clean," Jesus spoke to the leper. It was a good word. The leper was shackled by the heavy burden of his disease. He was rejected because of its contagion. Lepers were kept at a distance. Even family members were afraid to be near them. The cost had taken its toll on the man's mind as well. He knew what others thought of him, and he probably had the same feelings toward himself.

"If only I could be clean," he thought. Jesus knew. He knew the only thing that could restore the leper—that could give him a sense of purpose—was freedom from the bondage of his condition; to be cleansed. He said, "If the Son sets you free, you will be free indeed" (John 8:36).

Jesus wants you to be clean. He wants to liberate you from the fear of who you are—and what others may think of you. He wants to restore you to His image, to reclaim what the enemy has stolen: your sense of worth, your relationship with God. He wants to liberate you from your past. He wants to liberate you from the fear of your present. He wants to give you a hope for the future.

THE TOUCH OF TRANSFORMATION

"Immediately the leprosy left him." The leper thought his life was over. But then the hand of Jesus touched him. Jesus gave him a new beginning. He would be no longer the same. He was instantly transformed. Instantly, joy flooded his soul. In a moment, everything that held him down had been lifted from him. No, Jesus didn't free him from future pain; He just took away the immediate pain. No, the man who formerly had leprosy wouldn't be living on easy street; he would still have struggles, but he wouldn't have to face them alone—Jesus would be in his life.

Jesus wants you to know that joy. He wants to transform your life with His touch of forgiveness and restoration. He wants to give you a new determination. He wants to give you peace of mind, wholeness in your spirit. He wants you to reflect His holiness by living a life empowered by His Holy Spirit. "You will receive power when the Holy Spirit comes on you; and you will be my witnesses in Jerusalem, and in all Judea and Samaria, and to the ends of the earth" (Acts 1:8).

NEVER THE SAME

The next Sunday rolled around at our little church back in Ohio, and the crowd wasn't exactly standing room only. I thought there probably hadn't been enough advertising. Mark told me that there probably was—and that's the reason people stayed home! At any rate, I preached my first sermon that night. It was the first of thousands of sermons I've preached in small or large churches, in packed-out auditoriums, and even on television programs. I've never "recovered" from being touched by the Master. Truly, my life has never been the same. And truly, "I will never cease to praise Him."

Jesus Christ is the same yesterday
and today and forever.

—HEBREWS 13:8

On Christ the solid rock I stand,
all other ground is sinking sand.

—EDWARD MOTE

3

You Can Depend On Jesus

Terry Toler

You Can Depend on Jesus

By Terry Toler and Rusty Goodman

Often our faith
Is carelessly placed,
In empty words
That are spoken;
Don't be dismayed
When trust is betrayed,
And promises are broken.

Chorus

You can depend on Jesus,
You can depend on Jesus;
He is faithful and true,
What He says He will do,
You can depend on Jesus.

Tested and tried,
His word abides,
He is the rock everlasting;
And a building upon,
This cornerstone,
Will stand
While the ages are passing.

Bridge
> Forever He is the same,
> Trust in the power of His name.[4]

MY HERO

The late Charles "Rusty" Goodman of the legendary Happy Goodman Family was both a hero and mentor to me. Rusty, a Gospel Music Hall of Famer, was a great gospel singer and successful songwriter whose songs were recorded by artists ranging from Elvis Presley to Amy Grant. He is best known for penning the gospel classics "Who Am I," "I Wouldn't Take Nothing For My Journey Now," "Had It Not Been," and "Leavin' On My Mind." As a young boy, I would watch the Happy Goodman Family on television, and then I would pull out those old 78 rpm records and sing line for line with Sam Goodman, the tenor singer in the family.

In a youthful fantasy, I would get a phone call from the Goodmans asking me to fill in for Sam, who had a sore throat. If Sam ever did have a sore throat, I never knew about it—the call never came. Many years later, however, I would have the privilege of meeting Sam, Howard, and Vestal, and writing music with my hero, Rusty Goodman.

Terry

While pastoring in Ohio, my brother, Stan, and I were part of a mixed southern gospel group that traveled regionally and recorded several albums. The group included Mary Jane Carter, currently with the Pfeifers, Mary Jane's brother Phil, and Sonny Walters. It was a talented group, and I was truly blessed to be a part of it. The best thing about being in the group was its openness to try every new song I brought. As a result, our typical program was well-salted with my tunes.

One night the group, known as the Heritage Quartet, was the opening act for a big gospel concert in Southern Ohio that featured the Goodmans. That night as we finished our last song and headed off stage, Rusty, who had been listening in the wings, grabbed me by the arm and asked me if I had written the songs we used in the opening set. When I confirmed that I had, he said, "We need to talk during intermission." As eager as I was to hear the Goodmans, I was even more excited about intermission and the prospect of a personal conversation with this gospel music great.

A Jeremiah Moment

I was waiting stage left when Rusty exited, and in short order we found an outside door that led to a covered stairway and there began a conversation. Rusty looked at me and began what became a Jeremiah 29:11 moment in my life. Do you remember how the prophet Jeremiah spoke words of faith into the lives people who were fearful and uncertain about the future? Hear them again: "'For I know the plans I have for you,' declares the LORD, 'plans to prosper you and not to harm you, plans to give you hope and a future.'"

The prophet of God brought hope to the Babylonian exiles who had been ripped from their homes and found themselves in the grip of a hostile power. But God, who is always faithful, brought a word of hope to those helpless people and a promise so powerful they could begin to rebuild their lives upon it.

While I dare not compare my life at that time to that of the exiles, Rusty's encouraging words about my writing and the potential he saw for my songwriting became a life-changing encounter for me. My past experience with people in the music business had not been good. Disappointment followed every empty promise I had received from those who professed interest in my work. But this moment was different, and there was no one in the music business I respected more than Rusty.

Never underestimate the power of a well-timed word of affirmation. Not only was Rusty an encouragement to me, he also became an advocate for me in the publishing world. Within days of that intermission meeting, I was contacted by what was then the largest Christian music publisher in the world. Later I would learn that I was not the first young writer Rusty had sponsored, just one of his many protégés who have gone on to make significant contributions to the field of gospel music. Thus began my relationship with Rusty as my mentor and close personal friend.

A SONG FOR THE TIMES

In time Rusty and I started to write together. On one occasion in the mid 1980s, he and I got together in Oklahoma between solo appearances he was making to do some writing. Rusty had a special gift for divining the times musically and possessed a great sensibility about crafting a lyric in response to current events. Every song is born in a context, and "You Can Depend On Jesus" is no exception. In the early 80s, evangelicals entered satellite television broadcasting, which led to the meteoric rise of TV preaching. About that same time, evangelicals became a political power to be reckoned with. But by the mid 80s, a black cloud hung over many in the evangelical camp as some prominent leaders were caught up in hidden sins, bad judgment, and, in some cases, outright crimes. The secular media had a field day painting all evangelical leaders with a broad brush of scandal.

Rusty and the Goodman Family had met virtually all of the well-known media preachers, and he felt a personal pain and disappointment for those who had been swept away in a torrent of scandal. It was in this context that Rusty and I began a conversation about the need for Christians to focus attention on the One who never disappoints—the One who never leaves, the One who can be depended upon. We talked about the fickleness of people and how they are prone to say one thing and then do something altogether different. I can't really say who introduced the phrase "you can depend on Jesus," but it was precisely what we wanted to say in song that the people of God could sing. In fact, we agreed that the melody should be *Gaitherized*, meaning that a congregation should be able to sing it almost immediately upon first hearing.

Over the next day or so the song was crafted, and a few weeks later we went into a Nashville studio and made a demo. Not long afterwards, Rusty was diagnosed with a terminal illness, cancer. He succumbed to the disease in November of 1990. With Rusty's passing, the song was shelved, and it appeared that it would never be published or recorded.

Finally Recorded

Fast-forward to early 2007. My brother Mark and I were flying to Nashville to record the instrumental tracks for the long-awaited Toler Brothers project. When I say that is was long awaited, I don't mean to compare it to the latest Harry Potter book or a new gadget from Apple. There was no pent-up demand for the Brothers to do a project. The project was long awaited because it was something we three had talked about doing for years.

We had compiled a song list and had rehearsed (well, maybe *that's* a slight exaggeration) the basic arrangements of the tunes we were going to record. The producer, Michael Sykes, our longtime friend and one of Nashville's finest, had signed off on the song list and had secured an arranger to work with us the very next day. But somewhere on the evening flight between Oklahoma City and Nashville, I experienced a Holy Spirit moment and my memory was jogged about the song Rusty and I had written nearly twenty years earlier. The message of the song and the emotion of the memory came back to me in powerful ways. I pitched the idea of recording the song to Mark, and we decided that we had a quorum even without Stan! We decided then and there to record "You Can Depend on Jesus." As it turned out, the only significant change in the song was the addition of a bridge; otherwise we laid it down just as Rusty and I had written it two decades before. When the studio session players made their very first pass at the song, Mark and I both knew that our decision to include it was the right thing to do.

I'm not sure why it has taken so long for this song to be released. I don't know why

Jack (Stepfather) and Loretta (Mother)

Rusty never got the chance to record it. I don't know why, in the providence of God, a song written for a particular time would seemingly be so tardy in terms of getting to the church. But here is what I know: while men and women of prominence and obscurity continue to stumble and fall in every generation, there is One who is unchanging in His character and nature. His name is Jesus, and He never disappoints. I had a Bible professor who was fond of saying, "The eternal God has never broken one of His promises, and He's not about to ruin His reputation on you!"

The Unchanging One

In the second verse of "You Can Depend On Jesus," we used the metaphor found in Ephesians 2, where Paul writes about the chief cornerstone: "Consequently, you are no longer foreigners and aliens, but fellow citizens with God's people and members of God's household, built on the foundation of the apostles and prophets, with Christ Jesus himself as the chief cornerstone. In him the whole building is joined together and rises to become a holy temple in the Lord. And in him you too are being built together to become a dwelling in which God lives by his Spirit" (Ephesians 2:19–22).

A cornerstone is laid at the beginning of construction and establishes the foundation of a building. Everything that follows will rest upon this one stone. And Paul, using an architectural metaphor, says that Jesus is the cornerstone of the Church so that everything is built upon Him. Did you notice that the apostles and prophets rest upon Christ, the chief cornerstone? This is a timeless truth without an expiration date.

A colleague and I were discussing why so many people, including some that are highly competent and successful, resist change. We speculated on a variety of reasons why liberally educated people would sometimes exhibit spirited opposition to change. Our conclusion was this: competent people resist change because they fear change will render them less competent. I know this conclusion will not be published in a professional journal anytime soon—we may be the only two folk on the planet who agree on it! Yet that notion has become a source of great blessing to my soul. Our world has changed greatly since the beginning of recorded history, and in this twenty-first century things on planet earth seem to be changing at the speed of light. Yet I know there is a competent One, a changeless One, who has no fear of ever becoming incompetent or irrelevant! I celebrate the confidence that I place in Jesus Christ, who is always the same!

In introducing the song before a recent public performance, brother Mark said it best: "The more you depend on Jesus, the more dependable He becomes."

"And now, dear brothers and sisters, let me say one more thing as I close this letter. Fix your thoughts on what is true and honorable and right. Think about things that are pure and lovely and admirable. Think about things that are excellent and worthy of praise.

—PHILIPPIANS 4:8 NLT

We all need a daily check up from the neck up to avoid stinkin' thinkin' which ultimately leads to hardening of the attitudes.

—ZIG ZIGLAR

4

THINK ABOUT

Mark Toler-Hollingsworth

THINK ABOUT
By Terry Toler

Chorus

    Just think about (Just think about),
    What He's done for you (What He's done for you),
    Think about (Just think about),
    What He's brought you through (What He's brought you through);
    Think about the valleys low and deep,
    Think about the mountains high and steep;
    Think about rivers deep and wide,
    Think about the deserts hot and dry,
    Think about —Think about,
    Just think about what He's done for you.

    You may be tempted to shout I quit,
    I've felt that way—I must admit;
    Then looking to the cross of dark Calvary,
    I see that Jesus never gave up on me.

    Now you are tested—you'll surely come through,
    Shining like gold—better than new;
    Struggles are empty with no crown in sight,
    Yours is in view just keep holding tight.[5]

THE POWER OF THOUGHT

My brother Terry is a real intellectual. Don't quote me on this, but I think Terry was the model for that bronze and marble sculpture by Auguste Rodin called The Thinker. In this simple little song, Terry invites all of us to do some thinking. If you don't like where your life is headed, change the direction of your thought life. Wrong thinking will take you in the wrong direction; right thinking will take you in the right direction. It's just that simple. Proverbs 4:23 says, "Be careful how you think; your life is shaped by your thoughts" (GNB).

Philippians 4:8 encourages us to think about positive things. Some people just can't see the glass half full, right? You can show them the land of milk and honey, and all they will see are calories and cholesterol. The Bible says that we need to keep a guard at the gate of our minds, and that guard is God's peace. Philippians 4:7 says that "the peace of God, which surpasses all understanding, will guard your hearts and minds through Christ Jesus" (NKJV). We experience God's peace when we think right.

GUARDING YOUR MIND

Lots of folks these days live in gated communities, and guests must have a gate code to visit. (I live in a gated community, but this gate is more of a rusty fence; you have to get out of the pickup truck to open it). Be careful to whom you give the gate code of your mind. Don't let just any thought wander into your head. You have a right to deny access!

Did you know that the television in an average home is on for seven hours and seven minutes every single day? That's a lot of television! That means that if you live to be sixty-five, you will have spent over nine years of your life in front of the tube. Here is another statistic (or as we call em' in West Virginia, *satisics*): if you attend Sunday school every Sunday from birth to age sixty-five, you will have spent a little over four months of your life in Sunday school. Now make the comparison: nine years in front of the TV, or four months in Sunday school—which do you suppose is better for your mind?

Young Guns

You can't watch every movie that comes out just because it is "critically acclaimed." You can't read every book just because it's on the best-seller list. You can't listen to every song on the radio just because it is in the top forty. Second Corinthians 10:5 says, "We demolish arguments and every pretension that sets itself up against the knowledge of God, and we take captive every thought to make it obedient to Christ."

I admit that I am a real news hound. I read every newspaper I can get my hands on and watch every news program that I have time to watch. But most news is not good news; therefore, I must close the gate of my mind when it gets cluttered and overwhelmed with bad news. For example, sometimes the television news anchor will say, "We want to warn you, the images that you're about to see may be disturbing." I think they say that just to make you look all the harder, but for me it is a cue to shut my eyes or turn the channel to *The Andy Griffith Show*. The Apostle Paul gives us a pretty good checklist that we can use to size up the guests that want to enter the gate of our mind. It's found in Philippians 4:8. We should be asking them, "Are you true, honorable, right, pure, lovely, admirable, excellent, and worthy of praise? If not, then *scram!*"

God's Word is a wonderful filter for sifting out the filth that can bombard our minds. The psalmist said, "I have thought much about Your words, and stored them in my heart so that they would hold me back from sin" (Psalm 119:11 TLB). The Holy Spirit will help us think right and help guard the gate of our minds if we will simply submit our minds to Him. Romans 8:6 reminds us, "If our minds are ruled by our desires, we will die. But if our minds are ruled by the Spirit, we will have life and peace" (CEV). I'll take life and peace over death any day of the week.

ADDING GOOD THOUGHTS

Another important exercise for right thinking is reading—reading good books like my brother Stanley writes. That boy has written so many books I'm not sure he has ever had an unpublished thought! If Stan thinks about something for about five minutes, it'll probably turn into a book. Here is another fancy *satisic*: Americans spend more money on beer than on books. Maybe that explains why our bellies are bigger that our brains!

You say, "Books are expensive; I can't afford them." Guess what: here in America we have excellent public libraries that will actually loan you a book for *free*. Now that's in my price range!

I think every one of us can relate to the very first verse of Terry's song: "You may be tempted to shout I quit." Been there, done that! I could not tell you how many Monday mornings I have resigned from the ministry only to re-enlist by lunchtime. One of the greatest tactics of the enemy of our soul is to get us to quit. The trouble with many of us during those trying times is that what we're trying to do is give up!

The late Earle Nightingale, writer and motivational speaker, told the story about a boy named Sparky. For Sparky, school was quite a burden. He wasn't a very good student, failing everything from math to English. Sparky wasn't much of an athlete either. Socially, Sparky struggled to make friends. He never asked a girl out on a date for fear of rejection. There was one thing, however, that Sparky was really good at—drawing. He excelled in art. But in high school, no one was particularly interested in his artistic ability. During his senior year Sparky submitted a few cartoons to the yearbook editor, but they were rejected.

After graduating High School, Sparky pursued a career as a professional artist. He sent samples of his work to Disney, but again, they were rejected. Sparky decided to write his own biography through cartoons. The main character of the cartoon was a depiction of himself, a chronic loser and underachiever; it always rained on his parade, his kite would never fly, his friends called him "Blockhead" and he could never kick a football. But Charlie Brown won our hearts with his losing ways. Aren't you glad that Charles "Sparky" Schulz never quit?

And aren't you glad that Jesus never gives up on us?

REMEMBERING GOD'S POWER

The mind is powerful and capable of storing over one hundred trillion thoughts. That's amazing, especially in light of the fact that I've reached the point in life where I don't seem to remember things very well. I've got a mind like a steel whatchamacallit. I told my mother that I was having some memory trouble, and Mom, who knows more about pharmaceuticals than most druggists, told me to start taking Ginkgo biloba. I wrote down the name, but I forgot where I put the note. Weeks went by. Then one day I was wearing a suit I hadn't worn in a while, and I reached into the inside pocket and found the note with the reminder to buy the Ginkgo. I decided to strike while the iron was . . . how does that saying go? Anyway, I went right out and bought a bottle of Ginkgo biloba. When I got home and started to put this mind nourishing herbal supplement into the medicine cabinet, I discovered that I already had thirteen bottles of the stuff!

I love the faith, hope, and optimism of the second verse of "Think About,"

Now you are tested—you'll surely come through.
Shining like gold—better than new;
Struggles are empty with no crown in sight,
Yours is in view just keep holding tight.

Terry based a portion of this verse on Job 23:10, where Job says in the midst of his testing: "But He knoweth the way that I take: when He hath tried me, I shall come forth as gold" (KJV). Isn't that great? Instead of praying that God would remove the trial, Job had eyes of faith to see that God was refining him like gold through trials and tests.

I often wonder how many blessings and how much spiritual growth we forfeit because God answers our prayers to be removed from a test or the trial? First Peter 1:7 says, "These trials are only to test your faith, to show that it is strong and pure. It is being tested as fire tests and purifies gold—and your faith is far more precious to God than mere gold. So if your faith remains strong after being tried by fiery trials, it will bring you much praise and glory and honor on the day when Jesus Christ is revealed to the whole world" (NLT).

Do you remember the old Emergency Broadcast System (EBS) that they used to mention on television? You would be sitting there watching *Leave It to Beaver, Gilligan's Island,* or *Bonanza*—on second thought, we were never allowed to watch *Bonanza* because it was aired on Sunday nights. Lots of younger folk don't know this, but when the Toler Brothers

Tuxedo Time

were little, we had a drug problem—we were drug to Sunday school, drug to revival meetings, drug to Vacation Bible School, and we were even drug to church on Sunday nights!

Back to the EBS story. You would be watching your favorite show, and all of a sudden it would be inter-rupted with the words "This is a test. For the next sixty seconds, this station will conduct a test of the Emergency Broadcast System. This is only a test." Then there would be a blaring *Beeeep!* that lasted for a whole minute or two. My brothers would always challenge me to hold my breath during the whole *Beeeep!* I think they just wanted to see me turn blue.

One Christmas Eve the family was all gathered around the television watching the *Andy Williams Christmas Special* and eating some peanut brittle (which was kind of like watching grass grow while eating glass), and the EBS came on. I had a mouthful of peanut brittle, and as soon as the *Beeeep!* started, Stanley and Terry said, "Mark, hold your breath!" So with a mouthful of peanut brittle, I held my breath. After about twenty seconds, a sneeze came over me. I happened to be facing my brothers, bless their hearts, when the eruption came, and I sent them to the emergency room with shrapnel wounds.

James said, "Consider it pure joy, my brothers, whenever you face trials of many kinds, because you know that the testing of your faith develops perseverance. Perseverance must finish its work so that you may be mature and complete, not lacking anything" (James 1:2–4). Since we are human, we tend to forget that. When we were little boys, we used to sing one of Dottie Rambo's songs,

> Roll back the curtain of memories now and then,
> Show me where you brought me from
> And where I could have been;
> Remember I'm human, and humans forget,
> So remind me, remind me dear Lord.[6]

Journaling is a wonderful discipline that can help us remember God's faithfulness. Journaling serves as a written record of God's blessings, where He brought us from, and what could have been. It is a wonderful exercise to write down answers to prayer and lists of God's blessings on our lives. Think about what He has done for you; how He has brought you through the low valleys, the high mountains, the deep rivers, and the dry deserts.

Think about it!

May the words of my mouth and
the meditation of my heart be pleasing
in your sight, O LORD, my Rock
and my Redeemer.

—PSALM 19:14

Prayer makes the Christian's armor bright;
and Satan trembles when he sees the
weakest saint upon his knees.

—WILLIAM COWPER

5

SWEET COMMUNION

Stan Toler

SWEET COMMUNION
By Terry Toler

Early in the morning
My soul calls out to thee;
The day is long before me
And God knows what will be;
So as the sun brings the morning light
I meet the Lord in prayer,
And He assures me in the morning
He'll go with me through the day.

Chorus
Oh—what sweet communion,
With the Lord walking close beside along the way;
And if my feet should rush and get ahead
With love He will restrain,
Or if I should fall or lag behind
With love He prods again.
And oh what sweet communion
I enjoy through the day.

Through the day I'll encounter thieves,
Thieves who would rob and steal;

The joy I've found in Jesus,
This peace I've found so real;
So again I cry unto the Lord
And He's not far away,
And once again He manifests himself
And thieves just rush away.

Chorus
Oh—what sweet communion,
With the Lord walking close beside along the way;
And if my feet should rush and get ahead
With love He will restrain,
Or if I should fall or lag behind
With love He prods again;
And oh what sweet communion,
Oh what sweet communion,
Oh what sweet communion,
Oh what sweet communion,
I enjoy through the day.[7]

TIME TO COMMUNE WITH GOD

I like the story of the nine-year-old who set up a lemonade stand in front of his house. An economist was driving by and spotted the hand-lettered cardboard sign on the front of the stand that read, "Lemonade $5." The economist stopped the car and got out to talk to the young entrepreneur, "Son, even with inflation, that's quite a high price for lemonade." The nine-year-old quickly replied, "Mister, buy the lemonade if you want to, but please don't tell me how to run a business!" I admire the kid's spirit, but personally, I've never been afraid to ask for advice—especially God's advice.

As a teen I was challenged by my Sunday school teacher, Evelyn McFarland, to memorize a Bible verse. I took the challenge and memorized

Psalm 19:14: "May the words of my mouth and the meditation of my heart be pleasing in your sight, O LORD, my Rock and my Redeemer." Since then I have quoted that verse every day. It has provided incredible peace, comfort, and a positive outlook on my spiritual journey with Christ.

Over the years of speaking and teaching seminars internationally, I have built up enough frequent flyer miles to be bumped to first class for the Rapture! There are times when I have to catch an early morning flight. Some of them are so early that the roosters haven't even had time to clear their throat for a first crow. But no matter how early I rise or how late I get to bed, you can be sure that sometime during that day, I will have my time alone with God. I need His wisdom. I need His promises. I need His presence. And I find it all in my devotional time.

My brothers have made the same commitment. I'm proud of Terry and Mark. I've watched each of them as they have succeeded in life and ministry. Every time I hear Mark share a story or Terry sing a song (or vise versa), there is a smile of satisfaction on my face that's pretty tough to hide. Terry has written many award-winning songs, but one of my favorites is "Sweet Communion." It shows an amazing insight that God gave Terry—even when he was a teen—to express in song what He had whispered to Terry's heart. To me, this song is a pastor's song. And no matter where I go or what I do, I am always a pastor at heart.

I started pastoring when I was seventeen. In those early days, I'm sure some of my parishioners had weeks when they felt like taking me behind the woodshed and straightening me out. And here I was, the senior pastor of their church! It was a very humbling situation, and I needed all the help I could get. The fact is, I still do. Over ten thousand sermons and forty years of pastoral ministry later, the sweet communion with God in prayer and Bible study still gives me spiritual strength and valuable insight I need to do Kingdom work. Here are my secrets for having rich fellowship with God each day.

CONFESSION

Living a Christian life is living a God-pleasing life. The Psalmist said, "I desire to do your will, O my God; your law is within my heart" (Psalm

40:8). So everything I do or say—or think—must line up with God's revealed will. This was modeled in the life of Christ (see Hebrews 10:7 for more on that). Communion with God in prayer is a confession of our confidence in His power and in His promises. In other words, I pray and read the Bible because I believe that whatever God says He will do, He'll do. There is no interference in God's signal.

When I was young, my family didn't have cable television. In fact for a long time, we didn't have television at all! Later on we took ownership of a black-and-white TV with a twelve-inch screen, a horizontal control that was always on the fritz, and reception that that made every program look like a documentary about snow. And if the Alcoa Corporation hadn't invented aluminum foil, we wouldn't have had any reception at all! We wrapped the rabbit-ear antenna in foil to try to pick up a faint signal from the nearest television station. Moving the rabbit ears helped, but we just about got carpal tunnel syndrome trying to watch Mighty Mouse cartoons on Saturday morning.

Confession in prayer keeps the signal strong. I believe God hears me when I pray. And I believe He will answer my prayer according to His purpose for my life. As Terry said in his song, "If my feet should rush and get ahead with love He will restrain." So "sweet communion" is a SOLID communion. And every act of communicating with Him is linked to His authority and superiority. Confessing that is the foundation for praying Psalm 19:14. But how does it play out in my life?

EXPRESSION

I'm told there are over 450 thousand words in the dictionary and nearly seven thousand human languages and dialects.[8] So when someone tells you that they were left "speechless," you know they haven't been doing their homework. Yet you probably know someone who shouldn't have done their homework. Their words—sometimes insidious—are used as weapons of mass destruction. They randomly toss them around, resulting in wounded hearts and minds or the death of dreams and ambitions.

Now you can imagine when I get together with the brothers, the communion isn't always that sweet. Brothers usually don't spend a lot of time complimenting each other—ribbing and teasing is much more typical. There have been episodes in Oklahoma City restaurants when onlookers might have thought they were audience members for a "roast" at someone's retirement dinner. From put-downs to one-ups, the comments zip around the table like a scorpion on a hang glider. Everything is fair game, from hairstyles to shoe styles, and from preaching habits to sports team preferences.

Mark is usually the emcee at these brotherly barbecues. God has gifted the younger son with an incredible sense of humor. He has the ability to see the silly in almost every situation. He also sees the serious in what some think is silly. In fact, his ministry is

Mark in the Studio

marked by sensitivity to the spiritual and material needs of others as evidenced by the outstanding compassionate ministries emphasis at his church. Mark's humor spreads through our gatherings faster than a cough in kindergarten. Before we get to the main course of the meal, the brothers have already had a howl over some ridiculous story—usually "evangelistically stretched" to the breaking point. When the joke telling starts in earnest, we often race each other to the punch line—and Mark usually wins.

Words are wonderful ways to communicate our feelings. That's why it so important that our words line up with God's Word, the Bible.

It's tough being a positive influence in a negative world, but it can be done. You need God's help with your expressions throughout the day. The words you use to express what's on your mind can build up or tear down, almost instantly. Pray that they may build up.

REFLECTION

Our thoughts may be the most vulnerable of all areas of our life. We live in a communications age, but that hasn't necessarily improved our quality of life. Much of what is communicated should come with a warning: "Caution! These thoughts may be hazardous to your soul." Terry's song speaks about it: "Through the day I'll encounter thieves, thieves who would

Live at Trinity

rob and steal; the joy I've found in Jesus, this peace I've found so real." Satan, the enemy of our faith, would like nothing more than to destroy our focus on Jesus. He wants to creep into our thoughts and plant seeds of lust or greed or revenge. He is a thief who wants to steal our peace of mind.

A holy heart is the fortress of the soul. Jesus warned, "For out of the heart come evil thoughts, murder, adultery, sexual immorality, theft, false testimony, slander" (Matthew 15:19). A heart that is cleansed and filled with the Holy Spirit is one that is able to focus on Christ and stand against the thought attacks of the enemy. Matthew 5:8 says, "Blessed are the pure in heart, for they will see God."

So commit your heart completely to God, and start your day with God thoughts. Have some sweet communion with Him in Bible reading and prayer. You'll be amazed at how a mind filled with God's Word will guide your thought life.

Adoration

The Bible says "Give thanks to the LORD, for he is good; his love endures forever" (1 Chronicles 16:34). Devotional times are enriched by spending time telling God how great He is. You don't have to pose like a four-star general or talk like a fifth-year bishop to get God's attention. I believe heaven hears even the prayers of preschoolers when they say, "Now I lay me down to sleep, I pray the Lord my soul to keep." Authentic prayer comes from a heart that is honest and trusting. The truth is, people have to learn how to doubt God; trust is factory installed.

Notice these lyrics: "Again I cry unto the Lord, and He's not far away." God's proximity is a great motivator to commune with Him in prayer. No matter the circumstance, no matter the opposition, the Lord's presence brings a sense of soul rest.

In my book *Lead to Succeed*, I tell the story of an airplane that faced sudden turbulence. The copilot walked into the passenger section and explained that they were having a problem with one of the engines, but he assured them that the other three engines were working. As he went back to the cockpit he suddenly turned around and said, "Oh, I almost forgot. You'll also be relieved to know that we have three pastors on board this flight." One of the passengers turned to another and said, "I don't know about you, but I'd just as soon have four good engines."[9]

I don't know about you, but I'd just as soon have my Rock and my Redeemer" on board. "So as the sun brings the morning light I meet the Lord in prayer, and He assures me in the morning He'll go with me through the day."

How great is the love the Father
has lavished on us, that we should be called
children of God! And that is what we are!
The reason the world does not know us
is that it did not know him.

—1 JOHN 3:1

I do not want to merely possess a faith;
I want a faith that possesses me.

—CHARLES KINGSLEY

6

ONLY CHILD

Terry Toler

CHILD OF THE KING

By Cindy Walker

Praise God, Praise God, I'm a child of the King.[10]

ONLY CHILD

By Terry Toler and Vic Clay

My father has a great big family,
And there are many children besides me;
If you wondering how He divides His time,
Just let me say I never stand in line.

Chorus

He loves me like I was His only child,
Never felt so loved before,
I could never ask for more;
He loves me like I was His only child,
God really loves me,
Yes He really loves me,
He loves me like I was His only child.

He never favors me above the rest,
Yet I can't help but feeling that I'm blessed;

Blessed greater than rest I often say,

But then all the Father's children feel that way.[11]

ALL IN THE FAMILY

The Toler Brothers were blessed to grow up in a loving if imperfect family. We were more dysfunctional than some but more functional than most. Our dad and mom, and later our stepfather, each had the capacity to make each of us feel special. Though there were three of us (yours truly being the compliant middle child) our parents made every effort to let each one know that there was no difference in how they felt about us or in the way they cared for us. At Christmas, birthdays, and other occasions, they would spend an equal amount on gifts for each of us and let it be known that they would never knowingly show any difference between us.

This egalitarian parenting style included discipline. Mother was the chief disciplinarian at our house, and scissors and shears were her favorite tools for meeting out punishment. Now before you call the 800 number for Child Protective Services, let me explain. Mother, in addition to her other household duties, was our barber—hence the scissors and shears. The way this unique judicial system worked was highly personal and astonishingly effective. The length of our hair and the patterns of our behavior were inextricably linked. When we were well-behaved our time in "Judge Judy's" barber chair would be short and sweet. However, when we had spent too much time in proximity to Mom's last nerve, we would remain *in the chair* until we had *no hair!* These days we can get out old family photo albums and tell who was in trouble with Mom just by looking at the haircuts.

Perhaps one of the major reasons the three of us remain best friends is the absence of parental favoritism and sibling rivalry during those critical years of our human development. I don't think any of us has ever struggled in knowing that we were loved and accepted in our family, and that acceptance was based on who we were not what we had done. We were born into the family. We are Tolers—this is our identity. There is no need for a DNA test; we know who we are.

The Family of God

Early on in our lives, we were introduced to another reality: the place of all believers in the family of God. Much of our early theological education came through music. One of our Dad's favorite songs expressed it so clearly that even our young minds could comprehend what it meant to be a "Child of the King." That song was written in the nineteenth century by Harriet Buell and John Sumner. In fact, it was the very last song Dad sang in church before his young life was cut short by a tragic construction accident. I still have the lyrics committed to memory and have the lasting gift of the knowledge that Dad's last song ended with this testimony: "With Jesus my Savior, I'm a child of the King!"

Terry in the Studio

In the 1960s this theme was revisited and made popular by the First Family of Gospel Music, The Speer Family. Their rendition of Cindy Walker's composition, also titled, "Child of the King," was a favorite at our house. We would sing it in the car, obviously before CD players and satellite radio services were available. When the Toler Brothers got ready to record "Only Child"—a song that takes yet another look at the fatherhood of God and what it means to be a part of His incredible family—we just had to add the introit of the old Speer classic to the arrangement and pay tribute to them and their wonderful influence on our lives.

God's Amazing Grace

Beyond the nostalgia, this truth is sound both biblically and theologically. John writes: "But as many as received Him, to them He gave the right to become children of God, even to those who believe in His name: who were born, not of blood, nor of the will of the flesh, nor of the will of man, but of God" (John 1:12–13).

Later in life, and through formal theological education, I apprehended the truth that the believer's position as a child of the King is solely a result of God's amazing grace. The position of the believer is neither initiated nor maintained because of anything we can do to earn our position in the family. Nonetheless, because of our gratitude for our gracious adoption into the King's family, we can sing with the song writer, "All glory to God, I'm a child of the King!"

Author Eugene Peterson paraphrased the writing of John the evangelist in this way, "What marvelous love the Father has extended to us! Just look at it—we're called children of God! That's who we really are. But that's also why the world doesn't recognize us or take us seriously, because it has no idea who he is or what he's up to" (1 John 3:1 MSG). John says we are children of God—that is who we are. Saving grace is in our DNA. We are God's own children.

OUR RESPONSE

It was William Barclay who said, "It is by nature that a man is the creature of God, but it is by grace that he becomes the child of God."[12] It would be fair to protest his statement and hold that all men, women, boys, and girls are God's children. There is certainly some degree of truth to that idea that all people are full image bearers of God. But Barclay makes the case that there is a fundamental change in relationship when God calls and men, women, boys, and girls answer his call to salvation.

Barclay writes, "There are two English words which are closely connected but whose meanings are widely different, paternity and fatherhood. Paternity describes a relationship in which a man is responsible for the physical existence of a child; fatherhood describes an intimate, loving, relationship. In the sense of paternity all men are children of God; but in the sense of fatherhood men are children of God only when he makes his gracious approach to them and they respond."[13]

Have you ever heard or said yourself, "I could just tell that the person was a Christian by looking at them?" In other words, I can spot those who are "in the family." I confess that I have held such a presumptive position—and I have been wrong. We would like to be able to recognize the children of God just by looking at the outside, but it is not a very reliable means of discerning if someone is in the family of God. The Toler Brothers share some similar characteristics, and most observers will correctly guess that we are related. Yet those who are children of the King do not always look alike—at least to human eyes.

An Unlikely Sister

Some time ago I had an experience that convicted me of my weakness for judging those who do not appear to be in the family of God. It was the middle of a cold winter weekday afternoon when I saw her make her way up the steps of the church where I was pastoring. She was a middle-aged woman, doughty and unkempt. She was wearing what at one time was a white overcoat. Even from a distance, the coat looked stained and dirty. Up close it was worse. She grasped the railing with one hand and maneuvered a crutch with the other hand as she ascended the steps just outside my office.

I didn't go through a period of due diligence before judging her; there was not time to vet the facts. I simply knew that she was not one of us. I must confess I passed judgment on her without even knowing her name. But I did know her trade. I'd seen scores like her; serial beggars—people who go from church to church asking for money. Weekly and sometimes daily I would deal with her kind. They would tell stories of family deaths, lost bus tickets, and robberies. They would show me scars and describe illnesses that even doctors didn't have names for. I had heard it all, and yet I tried to help every one of them spiritually and materially—knowing that that their stories were usually delusions if not outright fabrications. I'm a bit ashamed to say it, but I figured her crutch was merely a prop for telling a story I was sure to have heard a thousand times before.

Still, I met her in the hall, greeted her, and asked if I could be of help. She said her name was Mary and that she needed to talk to a pastor. I invited her into my office, and she started telling me her story. But she never seemed to come around to asking for money. The more she talked,

Session leader Gary Prim, Terry, Producer Michael Sykes, Mark

the more I was intrigued by her. Mary was very articulate and seemed extremely bright. Finally I couldn't stand the mystery any longer and I asked her a leading question. "Where did you attend college?" She was indeed a college graduate and had earned a master's degree in piano performance. I was not sure what part of her story was fact and what might be fiction. Ultimately it didn't matter; she needed some food and a little cash. I helped her on both counts.

I asked Mary if she was a believer, and she said she was. I prayed with her, and she got up to leave. My office was just adjacent to the sanctuary, and she started toward the exit, stopped, and then looked through one of the door lights of the sanctuary. She said, "Is there a piano in there?"

"Certainly," I replied.

She said, "I haven't touched a piano in ages. Do you suppose I could play for a few minutes?"

"Absolutely," I said. I led her to the platform and she negotiated the steps and finally laid her crutch down beside the piano. It was just Mary and a beautiful grand piano; like two old friends who hadn't seen each other in a long time.

Then Mary started to play: Beethoven, Bach, and Mozart. I know that's what she played because she announced the composers. It was simply magical! Somewhere from deep within this unlikely human well a stream of wonderful music flowed forth and left me misty-eyed and speechless.

Her dirty, crusty fingers danced up and down the keyboard with remarkable precision. In my life I have had the good fortune of knowing and working with some of the finest musicians in Christian music. But I have never had a more incredible musical moment in my life than I had that day with Mary—the unlikely virtuoso. Finally she said, "Do we have time for the 'Minute Waltz?'" She winked and said, "You know it only takes a minute."

I applauded her performance and almost immediately mourned my own. She left. I would never see her again. Yet the experience lives on in my mind as a cautionary tale about judging a book by its cover. It was Saint Augustine who said, "God loves each of us as if there were only one of us." Mary was a one of a kind. What a privilege it is to be in the family—a diverse, unique, incredible family—with a father who loves each of us like we were his only child.

We are workers together with God.

—2 Corinthians 6:1 (NCV)

The church is like Noah's ark: it's filled with creatures of all kinds. Sometimes it gets a little stuffy and stinky, but in the end it's still the best thing afloat.

—Talmadge Johnson

7

ROLL ON CHURCH

Mark Toler-Hollingsworth

ROLL ON CHURCH

Chorus

    Everybody pull together
    And Let the church roll on (Roll on church)
    Let the church roll on (Roll on church)
    Let the church roll on (Roll on church)
    Everybody pull together (Everybody pull together)
    And let the church roll on (Roll on church)

    There's an usher in the church
    And he "ushes" wrong
    (What shall we do?)
    Teach him how to do it right
    And let the church roll on (Roll on church)

Chorus

    Let the church roll on (Roll on church)
    Let the church roll on (Roll on church)
    Everybody pull together (Everybody pull together)
    And let the church roll on (Roll on church)

    There's a steward in the church
    And he "stews" too much

(What shall we do?)
Let him stew until he's through
And let the church roll on (Roll on church)

Now there's a preacher in the church
And he preaches way too long
(What shall we do?)
Shape him up or ship him out
And let the church roll on (Roll on church)

There's a woman in the church
And she talks too much
What shall we do?
If you have a woman in the church
And she talks too much
There ain't nothin' you can do
But let the church roll on!

A Good Old Song

I love the song "Roll On Church" for several reasons: first, on the Toler Brothers CD *He Still Speaks*, this song features me! Being the baby of the family, I've never been shy about being featured. Second, I love the church humor of this old song. We really don't know who authored this song, but whoever wrote it certainly had a handle on the goings on in the church. There have been many versions of this song, and it has been recorded by everybody from Lester Flatt and Earl Scruggs to the Carter Family. Everybody puts their own bend to the song, especially the three preachers/part-time singers called The Toler Brothers. I even came across this version from *American Negro Songs*.

Hypocrite in the church, now that ain't right
Now what you goin' to do
Put him out, put him out

Let the church roll on
Backslider in the church, now that ain't right
Now what you goin' to do
Put him out, put him out
Let the church roll on.[14]

LEARNING TO LAUGH

The third reason I love and relate to this song is that I'm a pastor. If something can go wrong in the church, I have seen it happen. And when something does go wrong, you might as well see the lighter side of it. As someone has said, "If you can laugh at it, you can live with it." Trust me, I have seen my share of humorous things in worship services, board meetings, weddings, and even funerals. In my early days as a pastor, when things would go wrong I would say to myself, "One of these

Uncle Mark

days I'm going to look back on this and have myself a good laugh." Now that I have been a pastor for twenty-seven years, I say, "Why wait? Let's just have ourselves a good laugh right now!"

When Stan, Terry, and I were little boys we used to sing this song in children's church:

If we all will pull together, pull together, pull together,
If we all will pull together how happy we'll be;
For your work is my work, and our work is God's work,
So if we all will pull together how happy we'll be.

I wish you could have seen little Stanley do the motions to that song. The boy could have been on *Dancing With the Stars* (although that might put his ministerial credentials in jeopardy). Church work is happy work because it's God's work. But sometimes folks in the church don't pull their load, and then things get a little out of balance. Sometimes the singers won't sing, the teachers won't teach, and the ushers won't ush right. Then what do you do? I say, "Let the church roll on!"

I have a recurring Saturday night nightmare. It goes like this: I get to the church on Sunday morning, and the janitor hasn't cleaned the church. Last week's worship folders litter the floor and pews, all the tithe envelopes have been used for grocery lists and tic-tac-toe games. All the bathrooms are out of toilet paper—First John *and* Second John. Then the song leader calls and says his voice is feeling a little husky so he doesn't think he can make it to church that morning. The church pianist calls and says the in-laws from Leavenworth came in and she's probably not going to make it to church either. Every Sunday School teacher from the nursery to the Good Old Days class calls to say they won't be there to teach. To add insult to injury, my faithful head usher calls and says, "Pastor, I can't find my clip-on necktie, and I just wouldn't be found dead in the house of the good Lord without a necktie."

Now that's a nightmare!

ALL HANDS NEEDED

It didn't take me too many Sundays in the pastorate to figure out that it takes everybody pulling together to keep the church rolling on. Every pastor needs dedicated laypeople to keep the Sunday morning wheels from falling off. The pastor can't do it all and shouldn't do it all. I learned that lesson in my first church, where I tried to do it all. I unlocked the church, locked the church, cleaned the church, mowed the church lawn, led the prayers, led the singing, led every committee meeting, preached, and jiggled all the handles on the commodes before leaving the church at night. The result was that when I left that church, I left it paralyzed until they all pulled together and assumed responsibilities to keep the church rolling.

Church of the Nazarene General Superintendent Jerry Porter said, "Serving the Lord is fun, and getting funnier." Sometimes all you can do is shake your head and say, "Let the church roll on!" There is great comfort in knowing that the church is not ours but His. Jesus said in Matthew

16:18, "I will build my church. . . ." That takes the burden off the clergy and the laity. It is His church, and He will build it. However, 2 Corinthians 6:1 says that "we are workers together with God." We must pull together. Your work must become my work, my work must become your work, and our work must become God's work.

No Two Alike

God has uniquely gifted each of us to do His work. While He has called Stan, Terry, and me to be preachers, we all preach in the way that God has gifted us. To show you how God differs in the way He passes out even the same gift, think about this: Stan, Terry, and I have the same mother and father, we were all three born in the great state of West Virginia, and we were raised in the same house. We went to the same public school and the same private Christian university.

However, when it comes to the gift of preaching, we have different preaching styles. Stan and Terry are what I would call *gourmet preachers*. When they break the Bread of Life, they really know how to set the table! It is five stars, first class all the way. Stan and Terry will give you more utensils than you know what to do with; it is white linens and silverware every time. I, on the other hand, am a beans and cornbread preacher. It ain't much, but it'll fill you up! I've had gourmet meals, they are good, nice and dainty, but in a few hours later I am hungry and can't even remember what I ate. Brothers and sisters, when you've had beans and cornbread, you remember what you ate!

It takes all types to make the church roll on. God knows exactly what He is doing when He passes out His gifts to His people. Ephesians 4:11–16 (TLB) says this:

Some of us have been given special ability as apostles; to others He has given the gift of being able to preach well; some have special ability in winning people to Christ, helping them to trust Him as their Savior; still others have a gift for caring for God's people as a shepherd does his sheep, leading and teaching them in the ways of God. Why is it that He gives us these special abilities to do certain things best? It is that God's people will be equipped to do better work for Him, building up the church, the body of Christ, to a position of strength and maturity; until finally we all believe alike about our salvation and about our Savior, God's Son, and all become full-grown in the Lord—yes, to the point of being filled full with Christ. Then we will no longer be like children, forever changing our minds about what we believe because someone has told us something different, or has cleverly lied to us and made the lie sound like the truth. Instead, we will lovingly follow the truth at all times—speaking truly, dealing truly, living truly—and so become more and more in every way like Christ who is the Head of His body, the church. Under His direction the whole body is fitted together perfectly. And each part in its own special way helps the other parts, so that the whole body is healthy and growing and full of love.

FULL CAPACITY

It is up to every follower of Christ to discover, develop, and demonstrate their God-given gift in the church. That is what keeps the church rolling! It is important to note that gifts are received, not achieved. First Corinthians 12:11 says, "All these gifts have a common origin, but are handed out one by one by the one Spirit of God. He decides who gets what, and when" (MSG). We don't receive gifts because of any achievement; we receive them from a loving God who wants us to use them for the good of the church, and His glory. We in the church must discover our gifts, and we must also develop our gifts. A spiritual gift is not so much ability as it is a capacity to develop ability. Ability is a state of being, present tense. Capacity makes room for development, future tense. For example, God has given Stan, Terry, and me the gift of preaching. When we became His disciples, He gave each of us the capacity for preaching. We did not immediately begin preaching, although Stan did start preaching when he was fifteen years-of-age. Over the years God has helped each of us develop a capacity to preach; Stan recently preached his ten thousandth sermon!

Discover your gift, develop your gift, and most importantly—demonstrate your gift. That is what keeps the church rolling—people who actually use their gift. First Peter 4:10 says, "Each of you has been blessed with one of God's many wonderful gifts to be used in the service of others. So use your gift well" (CEV). When you don't use the wonderful gift God has given you, the church is robbed and hindered. Keep the church rolling by using well the gift God has given you.

When there is a lack of unity in a church, chances are, someone's not using their gift or worse yet, they are misusing their gift. Ephesians 4:16 says, "Under His direction the whole body is fitted together perfectly. And each part in its own special way helps the other parts, so that the whole body is *healthy and growing and full of love*" (TLB, emphasis added). Unified churches are healthy, growing, and full of love.

The last verse of "Roll On Church" is a verse we Toler Brothers have put our own bend on. The brothers have, on an occasion or two, pastored some dear sisters and brothers in the flock that have discerned that their spiritual gift is gossiping in the Spirit. It really isn't so much gossip to them as it is a "prayer concern." And as the verse goes, when you've "got a woman in the church and she talks too much, there ain't nothin' you can do but let the church roll on!"

Roll on church!

Jesus said to her, "I am the resurrection and the life. He who believes in me will live, even though he dies; and whoever lives and believes in me will never die. Do you believe this?" "Yes, Lord," she told him, "I believe that you are the Christ, the Son of God."

—JOHN 11:25–27

I believe in the sun when it is cloudy.
I believe in love when I do not feel it.
I believe in God when He is silent.

—STAN TOLER

8

I BELIEVE

Mark Toler-Hollingsworth

I BELIEVE

By Jimmy Fortune

When I see the sunrise in the morning,
When I feel the wind blow 'cross my face,
When I hear the sound of children playing,
I know its part of God's amazing grace.

Chorus

I believe there's a place called heaven,
I believe in a place called Calvary,
I believe in a man whose name is Jesus,
And I believe that He gave His life for me.

I wasn't there the day my Dad went to heaven,
Couldn't hold his hand as he closed his eyes to sleep,
But I felt the power of ten thousand angels,
Take his soul away to be crowned at Jesus' feet.[15]

THE POWER OF BELIEF

After our family moved from the small town of Baileysville, West
Virginia, to the big city of Columbus, Ohio, we noticed that people went

to the dentist. You may not have known this, but the toothbrush was invented in West Virginia. That explains why it is called the toothbrush; had it been invented in any other state in the union it would have known as the *teeth*brush. Even though Mom had store-bought teeth, she reasoned that since we were now bona fide city slickers, her boys ought to pay a visit to the dentist. Trust me, I needed to see a dentist; my teeth were so bad that my own hillbilly brothers called me Snaggletooth. Please forgive me, I should not have referred to Stanley and Terry as hillbillies. I should have been a little more politically correct and called them Appalachian Americans.

Nonetheless, it was in the waiting room of the dentist's office that I discovered the joy of reading. Back in those days, the company that produced *Highlights* children's magazine also published an interactive guide called *Think and Do*. What we believe impacts not only the way we think but also the things we do. What do you believe? What do you believe about God? What do you believe about Jesus Christ? What do you believe about the

Uncle Stan

hereafter? Accurate or not, what you believe about all of those things will determine your attitude, your behavior, your future in this life, and ultimately your destiny in the life to come. Beliefs are the foundation on which our lives are constructed. We always act according to our beliefs, even if those beliefs are false. For example, when I was a little boy my ornery older brothers convinced me that we had monsters in our basement. It wasn't true, but every time I had to make a trip to the basement I would get afraid; I would break out in a cold sweat, and the adrenaline would start pumping. That's why it is so vital that your beliefs are founded on truth.

Our Legacy of Faith

Perhaps the driving force for the *He Still Speaks* recording project was the desire of the Toler Brothers to leave a legacy. We wanted our children, and our children's children to know what is important to us. We wanted to communicate to every generation of Tolers, "This is what we believe, this is what we value, and this is what is near and dear to hearts." The recording was a tangible way of leaving our legacy of love. We wanted to communicate that we love Jesus, we love the church, we love family and friends, we love Gospel music, and we love life—and the best is yet to come!

Brother Terry wrote most of the songs on the project, and he also introduced Stan and me to a song written by Jimmy Fortune. Jimmy sang tenor with the Statler Brothers for twenty-one years. Perhaps his most loved and recognized song is "Elizabeth." In 2005 Jimmy released a Gospel song that he had written called "I Believe." When Terry gathered Stan and me around his kitchen table to listen to the song, we felt we had to record it. It not only tells our story but also powerfully and simply states what we believe.

John Wesley, leader of the Methodist movement in the late eighteenth century, constructed a method that is most helpful when it comes to formulating one's beliefs. Theologians and other really smart people refer to it as the Wesleyan Quadrilateral because Wesley made use of four authorities when coming to conclusions about what he believed. The four authorities are—

- *Scripture*—the Holy Bible, both the Old and New Testaments
- *Tradition*—the time-honored teachings of the Church
- *Reason*—rational thinking and sensible interpretation
- *Experience*—one's personal journey of faith

What Wesley believed about the Christian faith was revealed in Scripture, illumined by tradition, confirmed by reason, and lived out in personal experience. While the Scriptures are the sole source of truth, tradition forms a lens through which we view and interpret them. Both Scripture and tradition must be balanced and tested by reason and experience. Just as a chair has four legs to stand on its own, our beliefs are supported by the four "legs" Scripture, tradition, reason, and experience.

A FIRM FOUNDATION

Speaking of Scripture, I love the story of how Tiny had gotten saved and was invited to attend an old fashioned Wednesday night prayer and praise service. The pastor asked folks to stand and quote their favorite Bible verse, and one dear saint quoted the "Bible in a nutshell" verse, John 3:16: "For God so loved the world, that he gave his only begotten Son, that whosoever believeth in him shall not perish, but have everlasting life" (KJV). Another quoted the Golden Rule from Matthew 7:12: "Therefore all things whatsoever ye would that men should do to you, do ye even so to them: for this is the law and the prophets" (KJV). One dear brother who had forgotten to take his Ginkgo biloba racked his mind trying to think of a verse. He finally came up with one, stood to his feet and proudly proclaimed, "John 11:35: 'Jesus wept.'"

Encouraged by the expert Bible knowledge of his new found brothers and sisters in the faith, Tiny thought he would give it a try. So he proudly stood to his feet and declared, "I'm not sure where in the Bible it's found, but I like the verse that says, "Treat yourself to the best." A not-so-holy hush filled the room. The pastor looked at Tiny like a calf looking at a new gate. If you are an Appalachian American yourself, you know that Tiny didn't get his verse from the Bible; he got it off the side of a barn! The complete saying goes, "Treat yourself to the best. Chew Mail Pouch tobacco."

It is good for us from to revisit our beliefs from time to time. The Apostle's Creed, which summarizes our Christian beliefs, was developed during the early centuries of the church. It states:

I believe in God, the Father Almighty, Maker of heaven and earth; And in Jesus Christ, His only Son, our Lord: who was conceived by the Holy Spirit, born of the Virgin Mary, suffered under Pontius Pilate, was crucified, died, and buried; He descended into Hades; the third day He rose again from the dead; He ascended into heaven, and sitteth at the right hand of God the Father Almighty; from thence He shall come to judge the living and the dead.

I believe in the Holy Spirit, the holy Church universal, the communion of saints, the forgiveness of sins, the resurrection of the body, and the life everlasting. Amen.

FATHER AND SON

Do you believe in God, the Father almighty, maker of heaven and earth? Some people struggle to believe that God really exists. I love the old story about a saintly lady sitting on an airplane reading her Bible. A brash young college student seated next to her asked, "What are you reading?"

She kindly replied, "The Bible."

"You really don't believe the Bible, do you?" the student asked.

The saint said, "I believe every word of it from Genesis to Maps!"

The college student said, "Well, I'm an atheist. I don't believe any of it. I mean, do you really believe those far-fetched stories like Jonah and the whale?"

The dear lady humorously replied, "I know that story is a little hard to swallow, but yes, I believe the story of Jonah and the whale."

The young man said, "What about Daniel in the lion's den?"

"Yes," she said, "I believe that one, too. But I will admit that there are a few things I want to ask Daniel when I get to heaven."

The student asked, "What if Daniel didn't go to Heaven? What if he went to the other place?"

To that, the quick-thinking Bible scholar said, "Then I guess you'll have to ask him."

Psalm 53:1 declares, "Only a fool would say, 'There is no God!'" (CEV). How can we know that God exists? How can we know what He is like? Jesus said, "Anyone who has seen me has seen the Father" (John 14:9). Jesus is God personified. John 1:14 records, "The Word became a human being and lived here with us. We saw His true glory, the glory of the only Son of the Father. From Him all the kindness and all the truth of God have come down to us" (CEV). I believe in God because I believe in Jesus, His Son.

The chorus of Jimmy Fortune's song says, "I believe in a man whose name is Jesus, And I believe that He gave His life for me." As I pen these thoughts, it is the sacred season of Advent. I believe the Christmas story, from the cradle to the cross. I believe Jesus was born in Bethlehem, and I believe that He died at Calvary for you and for me. As I retell the Christmas story to my congregation, I find it imperative to convey the message—not only the fact that Jesus came but also why He came.

I've often wondered what it might have been like if Jesus came in our day. It is likely that He would have been considered a criminal. Someone has said that the FDA would have fined Him for turning water into wine without a license, not to mention feeding five thousand people without some sort of health inspection! The EPA would have been up in arms over Jesus' assault on fig trees. The AMA would have been after Him for practicing healing without a medical license. The NEA would have thrown the book at Him for teaching without a certificate. The NOW would have called a press conference condemning Jesus for not considering a female apostle. The SPCA would have locked Jesus up for driving hogs into the sea (and, incidentally, creating the original "Deviled Ham"). Last but not least, OSHA would have fined Him for walking on water without a life-jacket.

FAITH OF OUR FATHER

The Toler brothers adapted Jimmy Fortune's original lyrics of the second verse of his song to help tell our story. The verse goes,

I wasn't there the day my Dad went to heaven
Couldn't hold his hand as he closed his eyes to sleep
But I felt the power of ten thousand angels
Take his soul away to be crowned at Jesus' feet.

The reason our family moved away from the mountains of West Virginia was that Dad had hoped to find a better, safer way to make a living. In Wyoming County, West Virginia, there were two career options at that time: logger and miner. Both were dangerous jobs. Dad chose mining because that was what his father did and it was what his brothers did.

Mining is dangerous work even today, but you can imagine the safety conditions back in the 1950s and early 1960s. Dad was injured several times while working in the mines.

Some of Mom's brothers had gotten out of the mines and moved to Columbus, Ohio, to find construction jobs. They encouraged us to make the move. So like Jed, Granny, Ellie May, and Jethro, we loaded up the truck and moved to Columbus. It wasn't long before Dad got a job with a construction company. Just a few months later, he was killed in an accident on the job.

Ironically, the Wednesday night before Dad was killed, he sang in church, "A tent or a cottage, why should I care? They're building a palace for me over there"[16] Two days later, the Lord said to Dad, "Your mansion is ready, come on home." The headstone on our Daddy's grave reads, "Daddy waits for us in Heaven," and I believe he does with all of my heart. I believe it because Jesus said it. In John 14 He told His disciples, "Let not your heart be troubled: ye believe in God, believe also in me. In my Father's house are many mansions: if it were not so, I would have told you. I go to prepare a place for you. And if I go and prepare a place for you, I will come again, and receive you unto myself; that where I am, there ye may be also" (KJV).

Jesus said to Martha, "I am the resurrection and the life. He who believes in me will live, even though he dies; and whoever lives and believes in me will never die. Do you believe this?" (John 11:25–26).

Like Martha I say, "Yes, Lord, I believe!"

Then Jesus came to them and said,
"All authority in heaven and on earth
has been given to me. Therefore go and
make disciples of all nations, baptizing them
in the name of the Father and of the Son
and of the Holy Spirit, and teaching them
to obey everything I have commanded you.
And surely I am with you always,
to the very end of the age.

—MATTHEW 28:18–20

Evangelism is not a professional job
for a few trained men, but is instead the
unrelenting responsibility of every person
who belongs to the company of Jesus.

—ELTON TRUEBLOOD

9

THE SHADOW OF THE STEEPLE

Stan Toler

THE SHADOW OF THE STEEPLE

By Terry Toler and Rusty Goodman

Sunday mornin' sunshine
Bathin' the land,
Sunday mornin' people
With Bibles in their hands;
He wonders why they pass him by,
Walk around him on the street;
To shade the light that replaced the night,
He cups his hand to see.

The preacher talks about the needs in a distant land,
He says, "Folks are dyin' over there—
We've got to lend a hand;
It's getting' late—let's pass the plate,
Just do the best you can."
The congregation rises,
Somebody says "Amen."

Chorus
And in the shadow of the steeple
Someone's crying;
Does anybody care,

Can you hear him crying?
In the shadow of the steeple
Someone's crying.

A worn out coat he neatly folds
And puts in the place;
Where the shadow of the steeple
Will rest upon his face;
The choir sings—the church bells ring
And people homeward bound,
Just shake their heads—as they walk away
From the figure lying on the ground.

Chorus
And in the shadow of the steeple
Someone's crying;
Does anybody care,
Can you hear him crying?
Someone's out there dying,
Listen for their crying;
In the shadow of the steeple
Someone's crying.[17]

A POWERFUL STORY

Gardner Gentry is one of the best storytellers I have ever heard. I first heard him speak in 1972 during a pastors conference at Thomas Road Baptist Church in Lynchburg, Virginia. I come from a long line of West Virginia storytellers, so I knew midway through his first story that I was listening to a master craftsman.

The conference was life-impacting for John C. Maxwell and me. At the time, we were working together as a pastoral team at Faith Memorial Church in Lancaster, Ohio. We pooled our limited resources with Jack

Norman, David Cyrus, Alvin Conkey, and Paul Dorsey and drove to Lynchburg in a station wagon. The car looked exactly like the one movie character Clark Griswold drove in his pursuit of Wally World on one of his National Lampoon vacations. To make matters worse, all six of us stayed in one room at the Holiday Inn! We had more mattresses on the floor than a family of Yugoslavian acrobats in a bankrupt traveling circus.

During the concluding service of the great conference, gospel singer Doug Oldham sang "The King is Coming"—the classic gospel song written by Bill and Gloria Gaither. Goosebumps spread over the crowd faster than a case of chickenpox. The emotional tide was so high I heard a Presbyterian sitting near the back say "Amen" out loud! (And a Nazarene sitting near the front started to take up an offering.) What a service!

Then Gardner Gentry told the vast crowd of Christian workers the story of the growth and transformation of his Travis Avenue Church in Fort Worth, Texas. Gentry's story told of a boy named Cecil who had died in the shadow of the church's steeple and of how his death had motivated the church to reach its community for Christ. Needless to say, we left the conference motivated to win souls. Our church in Lancaster exploded in growth as a result.

After the conference, John and I decided to invite Gardner to come to the Mid-East Church Conference to speak, and we asked him to tell the story about Cecil. I invited Terry to attend the event, and he was so inspired he went home and wrote the first set of lyrics to "The Shadow of the Steeple." Later, Rusty Goodman and Terry rewrote the song, and the famed singing family, The Happy Goodmans, recorded it on their last CD, "Reunion."

Uncle Terry

There are fewer steeples to be seen these days. Once marking the cityscapes of North America like hands of hope reaching to the sky, steeples are now so uncommon that they become points of interest for out of town visitors. But the fact is people are still crying in the shadow of the steeple. Within footsteps of small, medium, or mega-sized churches, there are folks who are longing for hope and healing. At times I think the noise of our organizational machinery is so loud we can't hear them.

I remember trying to preach a sermon in my church in Florida while a little boy with a toy car was pretending to zip around the Daytona Speedway. The problem was he was at the front of the church, on his knees, facing the front pew. If you don't think its tough trying to pontificate on the Pentateuch while a preschooler is making *vroom! vroom!* noises out loud, give it a try! His toy car was breaking speed records on the straightaway of the pew, and I was trying to make a U-turn in a sermon on the platform. Needless to say, the little boy won the race, while I lost the attention of the crowd—and half of my patience.

We dare not allow organizational noise throw our churches off course. We need to keep listening for the crying. We can't be guilty of walking around with our Bibles in hand, ignoring the hurting. We have what the world needs: a message of hope through faith in the Lord Jesus Christ. A way to be forgiven of the past and to be certain of a future.

We have to stay the course. How?

Obeying the Master

Jesus didn't leave us steeple folk with many options when it comes to showing compassion on those around us: we must obey the master. One command rings in the ears of every child of God, in spite of the clanging noise of committee-ism: "Go and make disciples of all nations." Having grown up in the church, I have been to many missions conventions. Some of my earliest memories are of the missionary's delightful announcement: "Would someone get the lights." I knew as soon as the usher found the light switch—which never happened right away and often resulted in more lights being turned *on* rather than off—I would be transported across the seas by a slide presentation.

Frankly, my young heart was stirred by the sights and sounds. I dreamed about preaching the gospel in some of those far countries and usually awoke while the usher was trying to get the lights back on—and usually leaving half of us on the Dark Continent.

Afterward, my friends and I would crowd around the missionary's table of curios. There I would stick my finger in the mouth of a stuffed python, or try to play the "The Stars and Stripes Forever" on a flute carved out of a tree limb, or put the headdress of a medicine man on my head and pretend to heal the bully in my Sunday school class. And often I would join my friends at the front of the church after the missionary gave an invitation to those who would serve Christ as a missionary if they were called to do so. The call didn't immediately take me to those foreign lands; it happened later in my ministry. Now I have traveled to many of those same countries and preached the gospel.

And now I know the fire that was burning in the hearts of those dear servants of Christ. People everywhere need God's Word. They need to know of a Savior. Hearing the cries of those who live in the "shadow of the steeple" begins by listening to the voice of Jesus—and praying, giving, or going for the cause of world missions.

EMBRACING THE GOSPEL

I've played a lot of basketball in my time, but I've never been known much for slam-dunking the ball through the net—at least not without a stepladder. But I learned a long time ago it doesn't matter how tall you stand as long as you stand for something. And the something I stand for is the gospel: the good news of a salvation that was paid with blood by the sinless son of God on the Cross. Like the Apostle, I embrace the gospel. "I am not ashamed of the gospel, because it is the power of God for the salvation of everyone who believes" (Romans 1:16).

Like many of you, I've stood in the lineup of a children's church choir, waving like an idiot to my relatives and singing "Jesus Loves Me" as if I were auditioning for a Broadway musical. But one day the song became a reality to me. I invited Jesus into my heart, to be my Savior. Later on I was filled with His Holy Spirit and empowered to live a victorious Christian life. I embraced the gospel—and I haven't let go!

I believe that Jesus is the son of God sent from heaven.

I believe He lived a sinless life.

I believe He died on the Cross for me.

I believe He rose from the grave after three days.

I believe He ascended into heaven and will return to earth to take me to the place He has prepared for me.

I believe He sent His Holy Spirit to indwell, guide, and sanctify me.

We steeple folk need to stand for something. And I encourage you to be someone who will embrace the gospel, the truth of God's holy Word—the Bible. As the old saying goes, "if you don't stand for something, you'll fall for anything." Embrace the truth. It's another important step in developing a concern for those who are crying or dying in the shadow of the steeple.

LIVING THE GOSPEL

Awhile back I was traveling with a friend on a four-lane highway through the downtown of a large city. We were enjoying a conversation and making our way to the airport, where I was to catch a flight to Oklahoma City. Suddenly we were confronted by enough brake lights to illuminate the state of New Hampshire at midnight—during a blizzard. An accident on the road ahead instantly turned the pleasant drive into a motorized game of checkers. Cars and trucks were making their moves, trying to get to their destination by eliminating us! And truth be told, we had a few passing thoughts about "crowning" some of them!

At one point, Bubba in a diesel pickup slowed to make room for an eighteen wheeler to enter the one useable lane. We smiled, thinking this Samaritan in sunglasses would allow us to get by also. Wrong. He stopped momentarily, then sped up, giving us a nasty wave and a laugh as he closed the gap. As my friend, comedian and songwriter Aaron Wilburn, would say, "Bless his heart."

You've heard of tough love? I believe in it. It sure is tough to love some folks! But God has never created anyone He couldn't love. And we steeple fold can be filled with God's love to overflowing. The Bible says, "Oh, how generous and gracious our Lord was! He filled me with the faith and love that come from Christ Jesus" (1 Timothy 1:14 NLT). Someone in the shadow of the steeple needs to know God's love by your loving them. Live the gospel.

SHARING THE GOSPEL

The Toler brothers have probably been to enough church suppers to feed all the extras in a Star Wars video! With a combined seventy-five years in ministry, there isn't a fried chicken in the land that could fly by us. I'm usually a one-meal-a-day guy, but put me first in line at a potluck and I'll scare the daylights out of a green bean casserole! Yet there is something far more important than fried chicken and green bean casseroles. It is the spiritual food that feeds the soul.

Jesus told of a young man who tried to feed his hunger at the buffet table of the world: "There was a man who had two sons. The younger one said to his father, 'Father, give me my share of the estate.' So he divided his property between them. Not long after that, the younger son got together all he had, set off for a distant country and there squandered his wealth in wild living. After he had spent everything, there was a severe famine in that whole country, and he began to be in need . . . .When he came to his senses, he said, 'How many of my father's hired men have food to spare, and here I am starving to death!'" (Luke 15:11:17).

The world lied to the younger son. It promised plenty and left him with nothing. There is a hunger deep in the soul that cannot be satisfied apart from God. Steeple folk need to share the Bread of Life (John 6:35). And Jesus' parable is a call to duty.

> In the shadow of the steeple
> Someone's crying;
> Does anybody care,
> Can you hear him crying?
> Someone's out there dying,
> Listen for their crying. . . .

But while he was still a long way off, his father saw him and was filled with compassion for him; he ran to his son, threw his arms around him and kissed him. The son said to him, "Father, I have sinned against heaven and against you. I am no longer worthy to be called your son."

—LUKE 15:20–21

People are lonely because they build walls instead of bridges.

—JOSEPH NEWTON

10

THE PRODIGAL SON

Terry Toler

THE PRODIGAL SON
By Terry Toler

I still recall the day
His boy went away,
I remember his sad eyes could not conceal,
The hurt he felt down deep inside
Was too much for him to hide,
He waved good-bye—turned around and cried.

At first light you could find him
Lookin' out the window,
Wonderin' if he came home in the night;
At noon he'd set another place at the table,
He would breath a prayer and hope he was all right.

The evening sun was sinkin'
On the porch he set thinkin',
"Who's that comin' down the lane alone?
He looks so tired and weary
Now, I see him clearly,
It's my boy—he's finally comin' home."

They met in the yard
Both cryin' hard,
Their tears ran together like a stream;
The boy fell down to his knees
And cried, "Forgive me please
For all the wrong that I have done;
I'll just be your servant,
You won't even have to call me son."

Chorus

Then they danced together,
Called all the neighbors,
Celebrated his return;
Sang in sweetest harmony
That welcome home melody,
A son who was lost now is found;
They killed the fatted calf and placed a ring upon his hand
Dressed him in a brand new robe of royalty again;
The Father said, "You're welcome home,
Forgiven for the things you've done.
You can be my servant,
You can be my servant,
And my son."
I know this story oh so well
And it's one—that I love to tell
He is my Father
And I was that prodigal son.[18]

COMING HOME

By William J. Kirkpatrick

Coming home, coming home, Nevermore to roam!
Open wide Thine arms of love; Lord, I'm coming home.[19]

THE PEARL OF PARABLES

The Toler boys were reared in a great storytelling tradition. As children we would sit mesmerized as the elders would hold forth. Those who could spin long tales about—well, anything—were greatly admired in the coal mining community where we lived, down in the southwest corner of West Virginia. To this day, when our families get together, there is nothing we enjoy any more than telling stories.

Whenever Jesus wanted to get a message across, especially to those who loved religion, He didn't reel off a lengthy theological dissertation; He told a story. And what a master storyteller He was, ever surprising His listeners by making the true character and nature of God crystal clear to His listeners. In the trio of stories recorded in Luke 15, two of the three have not commonly been a source for songwriters. The stories of the lost sheep and lost coin have certainly been woven into songs, but their use is nothing compared to the prolific way the story of the lost son has found its way into musical expression.

Every songwriter worth his or her salt has attempted to set the "pearl of all the parables" to music. Not even the Vatican can provide a full listing of every song based solely or loosely on this story since it was first told. Even a cursory check of iTunes reveals an amazing list of "prodigal" offerings.

REAL-LIFE PRODIGAL

The primary inspiration of Scripture was sufficient for me in my humble writing effort on this subject. However, I did witness the journey of a modern-day prodigal that further motivated me to write "The Prodigal Son."

This human drama played out at about dusk on a sidewalk in a small farming town. There characters were the pursued, young man walking with certain defiant steps, and the pursuer, a man more than twice the age of the younger man. I knew them both. The young man was known by everyone in our small town. He had earned a reputation as a thief, thug, and troublemaker. Recently released from prison, he was placed on a short leash by the court, complete with a curfew and a variety of other limitations intended to help him to get his life on track—and to protect the general public.

On this night he was fleeing the rule of law, the warmth and comfort of home, and the very presence of his father. The pursuer was his father, a man with a sterling reputation, a gracious man—in fact, a gifted preacher of the gospel. Night after night he would stand in pulpits across the land and plead for sinners to return to the Father. And they would respond to his loving invitations—sometimes en masse. On this night he was pleading with his own son: "Please don't go, Son. You're headed for trouble."

The son looked over his shoulder and snarled, "I'm going, and there is nothing you can do about it."

It was a sad portrait of a rebellious son and a loving, pursuing father.

I was there to support my friend, the evangelist. And I would love to report that the boy came to his senses and stopped his wayward plight that very night. But on that particular night, the son ran away. I watched it all through the open window of a car and waited for my evangelist friend, who, after some time, reluctantly gave up the immediate pursuit of the boy. After that night was over, he continued to pursue the son he loved even more than his own life.

He followed him to crack houses.

He followed him to emergency rooms.

He followed him to the county jail.

He followed him to the court of law.

He followed him to a maximum-security prison.

And as far as I know, he is still pursuing him. The end of the story has yet to be written.

GOD THE PURSUER

Now from the pearl of parables, I want to make a connection to the Old Testament and to one of the most beloved passages of Scripture in all of holy writ, the Shepherd's Psalm, Psalm 23:

The LORD is my shepherd, I shall not be in want.
He makes me lie down in green pastures,
he leads me beside quiet waters,
he restores my soul.
He guides me in paths of righteousness
for his name's sake.
Even though I walk
through the valley of the shadow of death,
I will fear no evil,
for you are with me;
your rod and your staff,
they comfort me.
You prepare a table before me
in the presence of my enemies.
You anoint my head with oil;
my cup overflows.
Surely goodness and love will follow me
all the days of my life,
and I will dwell in the house of the LORD
forever.

I love the phrase "love will follow me." Some scholars believe that it is accurate to translate the word *follow* as pursue. The Father of all creation pursues men and women, boys and girls, reaching to them—letting them know just how much He loves them. He yearns that all should come to repentance. He yearns that none should perish. God is a pursuer!

A HAPPY ENDING

Perhaps you are still having a little trouble making that connection because of one troubling element of the parable of the lost son. In the case of the lost sheep, the shepherd goes out to pursue that one lost lamb. In a similar way, the owner of the lost coin suspends all to actively pursue it.

What about the father in the story of the rebellious son? Why didn't Jesus tell a story like the one I witnessed, a story of a father who actively pursued his wayward son?

When the prodigal of the parable had reached the dead end of "Pig Pen Road," he reflected on life at his father's house. He was able to run away from all he detested about his father's house. But as he sat there with the pigs, the memory of the love of his father caught up to him. Do you see it? He was pursued by the love of his father, even though his father never left home. Here is the heart of God, prodigals. He will pursue you, no matter where you go, no matter what you do. God is a pursuer.

Rehearsal

It was a happy ending when the lost lamb was found. I'm sure the first hearers of the story must have smiled from ear to ear. A lamb is valuable. And the discovery of the lost coin after an all-out search surely brought pleasure to listeners. But when Jesus told them about an ungrateful son who wished his father were dead, who shamed his family and sank into unspeakable degradation yet was met by a forgiving father, it must have been the worst ending they could have imagined. "A rebellious son is worthless!" they must have protested. What an outrage it must have seemed. To ice the cake, Jesus went over the top by telling how this father even ran to meet the returning son. And Jesus still wasn't through making his point. He has the father forgive the rascal and call for a feast to welcome home the son who was "lost" and now is "found."

Some time ago I was a guest in a church service where a powerful evangelistic message was proclaimed. When the invitation was given, something happened that I had never seen before nor since in my entire life. As men and women began to pour out of their seats into the aisles and make their way to the front of the church, the congregation began to applaud. In short order the sanctuary was filled with loud and sincere applause of praise. Since this church was not in the tradition that I am most familiar, I tried to divine what was really happening in that moment. I concluded that the congregation was, in their own way, joining in the celebration that goes on in heaven when one prodigal comes home. I will never forget that scene—a moment in time where earth and heaven were in harmony.

Here is the so what part of the story of the prodigal for me. Salvation is not so much about our badness as it is about God's goodness. Surely goodness and love shall follow me—pursue me—all the days of my life!

Finally, brothers, whatever is true,
whatever is noble, whatever is right,
whatever is pure, whatever is lovely,
whatever is admirable—
if anything is excellent or praiseworthy—
think about such things.

—Philippians 4:8

Jesus, the name that charms our fears,
that bids our sorrow's cease.

—Charles Wesley

11

What a Lovely Name

Stan Toler

What a Lovely Name
By Charles B. Wycuff

There's a name above all others,
Wonderful to hear, bringing hope and cheer.
It's the lovely name of Jesus,
Evermore the same, what a lovely name.

Chorus
What a lovely name, the name of Jesus.
Reaching higher far, than the brightest star.
Sweeter than the songs they sing in heaven,
Let the world proclaim, what a lovely name.

He'll return in clouds of glory,
Saints of ev'ry race, shall behold His face.
With Him enter heaven's city,
Ever to proclaim, what a lovely name.

Chorus
What a lovely name, the name of Jesus.
Reaching higher far, than the brightest star.
Sweeter than the songs they sing in heaven,
Let the world proclaim, what a lovely name.

Tag

>   Let the world proclaim, it'll always be the same
>   What a lovely name.[20]

THE HAPPY GOODMANS

There probably isn't a southern gospel music fan that hasn't heard the late and great Vestal Goodman sing. She had a voice that would rattle the CDs on the product table in the foyer. And her smile would warm the Arctic during a winter chill. When Vestal sang a song, you knew you'd been sung to.

The Goodman family of eight brothers and sisters started singing in the 1940s. After Vestal and Goodman brother, Howard, married, they began an itinerant evangelistic ministry. Soon they were joined by brothers Sam, Rusty, and Bobby, and they expanded their ministry to include "Singings" in churches and auditoriums. After an appearance at the National Quartet Convention in the 1960s, they soon became southern gospel favorites. They won their first Grammy Award in 1968 for their album *The Happy Gospel of the Happy Goodman Family*.[21]

I first heard the Goodmans in 1961 by means of a 78 rpm record player at my Uncle Earl's home in Oceana, West Virginia. The only "surround sound" the Toler family had back then was when we gathered around that Sears-and-Roebuck portable. Wondering whether the next record on the spindle would drop just added to the entertainment. As the needle scratched its way along the vinyl grooves playing Howard's testimony song, "I Wouldn't Take Nothing for my Journey Now," I thought I had died and gone to music heaven!

Apparently Dad and Mom agreed. They began taking us to every Happy Goodman Family concert within a hundred-mile radius. Mom loved Vestal's crystal clear voice, and our family soon began singing those contagious Goodman songs. Mom even got a beehive hairdo to match Vestal's!

The Goodmans would endear themselves to us in other ways as well. Award-winning songwriter Rusty Goodman heard one of Terry's songs when our Heritage Quartet (which included Mary Jane Carter, now with the Pfeifers) sang with the Goodmans. Rusty soon became Terry's mentor, helping to launch a songwriting career by getting him a contract with Word Music. Rusty and Terry even cowrote a few songs, including "In the Shadow of the Steeple" and "You Can Depend on Jesus."

In recent years Vestal has been known for her regular appearances on the Gaither Homecoming videos with her trademark white hanky in hand, and her husband, Howard, at her side. With trio member and accompanist Johnny Minnick at the piano and rows of well-known artists and friends behind her, Vestal would sing the heavens down. That dear woman had such charisma that I believe she could have squeezed a "Hallelujah!" out of an Episcopalian with two doctorates in biblical archaeology. When Vestal sang Charles Wycuff's song "What a Lovely Name," you felt like you were sitting in the presence of Jesus along with

Mary Jane Carter and the boys

her. The once-shy singer, who said God anointed her voice during a revival meeting, blessed millions of people with her Spirit-anointed performance of that song.

When the Toler Brothers were making plans to record their first CD, I knew "What a Lovely Name" had to be included. And when I heard the news that her niece, well-known gospel singer Tanya Goodman-Sykes, had agreed to sing along on the recording, which was produced by her husband, Michael, I whooped so loud I think Vestal heard me up there in heaven!

The name of Jesus is like silk and steel. Announced by heaven to the heart of Mary, it means "Jehovah Saves." The tenderness that revealed it is matched by the infinite glory and majesty that stand behind it. Jesus is the Lord of Lords who stepped from the throne of heaven to walk homeless on the earth. What a lovely name!

A NAME OF AUTHORITY

At encountering the name of Jesus, people have to make a decision. Over the centuries, various choices have been made. Jesus has been mocked by philosophers, banished by politicians, and snubbed by scholars. He has been evicted from schools and locked out of His own church. His name is used freely as an expression of rage even as laws are passed to prevent its mention in our courts. He has been banished from the season that celebrates His birth. To some, He is as the prophet said, "despised and rejected."

But there's isn't the last word! The Bible says of Jesus, "God exalted him to the highest place and gave him the name that is above every name, that at the name of Jesus every knee should bow, in heaven and on earth and under the earth, and every tongue confess that Jesus Christ is Lord, to the glory of God the Father" (Philippians 2:9–11).

One day His foes as well as His followers will stand before the glare of His crystal pure eyes and give an account of their lives. He slipped into the side door of earth as an unannounced king, but He will return as the Lord of Lords. His most powerful enemies will whimper at His feet and beg for the mercy He made available from the very beginning. There is authority in the name of Jesus.

Some time ago I was making a purchase using the credit card that helps me keep track of my travel expenses. I was shocked when that store clerk in Indiana swiped the card a couple of times and said, "Mr. Toler there is a problem with this card."

I replied, "No ma'am, there isn't a problem with that card. The account was paid in full last week. You can call the company to check."

She hemmed and hawed like a tax assessor evaluating the property of the governor's eldest child. Finally, she called the store manager and whispered into the phone. I stood at the counter smiling and wondering if my dear wife had bought a neighboring subdivision while I was away. Soon the explanation came:

"Mr. Toler, it seems that someone in Italy is using your name and card number to buy groceries at this very moment."

Using my name and account to buy groceries! Using my authority to authorize his or her purchases! I thought about it later on and realized that is exactly what the name of Jesus does for me. I face the daily ruts, rants, or riots in the authority of Jesus' name. I put the stuff of life on his account. His is the name above all others!

A NAME OF INFLUENCE

The disciples Peter and John were on their way to church one day, and on the church property, near the entrance door, they met a man who was begging money from passersby. He had been crippled from birth. He asked them for money, but the disciples had even less cash than a holiness preacher in a pioneer district. But their response suggests the influence of Jesus' name: "Then Peter said, 'Silver or gold I do not have, but what I have I give you. In the name of Jesus Christ of Nazareth, walk.' Taking him by the right hand, he helped him up, and instantly the man's feet and ankles became strong. He jumped to his feet and began to walk. Then he went with them into the temple courts, walking and jumping, and praising God. When all the people saw him walking and praising God, they recognized him as the same man who used to sit begging at the temple gate called Beautiful, and they were filled with wonder and amazement at what had happened to him" (Acts 3:6–10).

The Toler brothers have stood with parishioners in their churches as they faced some of the worst things life could offer. But each of us could tell you the difference that the mention of Jesus' name made on those occasions. Remember that moment in your life when the lovely name of Jesus brought you hope and cheer? His name is influential.

Russ Taff, John Pfeifer, and the Brothers

A Name of Security

I don't know if you've ever had a gathering of people vote on whether you would have a job the next week. If so, you're probably a pastor. In our denomination, the congregation either votes to keep you as pastor or rents you a U-Haul and piles your sermon notes in the parking lot for a going away marshmallow roast. For some, Pastoral Vote Sunday isn't necessarily "Friend Day."

Job security is always subject to the smiles or frowns of those in charge. And living in the twenty-first century is a bit dizzying at times. About the time you find a convenience store that is in a "gas war" with the filling station across the road, the filling station is demolished and a bank is constructed in its place. (And have you noticed that banks seem to multiply like plastic shopping bags?)

Security issues aren't limited to job sites, however. We're faced with security risks and security alerts almost every week. I've had to remove my shoes at airport security checks so often I've almost decided to paint my feet an oxford color!

When people talk about secure borders, I don't think they're just referring to national boundary lines. There is a worldwide need to feel there are protective fences around all of us, and not necessarily physical fences. We need emotional and spiritual fences as well. Everything is changing. Here's some good news: "Jesus Christ the same yesterday, and to day, and for ever" (Hebrews 13:8).

"Evermore the same, what a lovely name." No wonder the smile on Vestal's face when she sang this song. No wonder the tears of joy that chased each other down her cheeks. No wonder the standing ovations. No wonder the shouts of praises. No wonder.

"Let the world proclaim, what a lovely name."

The heavens declare the glory of God;
the skies proclaim the work of his hands.
Day after day they pour forth speech;
night after night they display knowledge.
There is no speech or language
where their voice is not heard.
Their voice goes out into all the earth,
their words to the ends of the world.
In the heavens he has pitched a tent for the sun,
which is like a bridegroom coming forth from his pavilion,
like a champion rejoicing to run his course.
It rises at one end of the heavens
and makes its circuit to the other;
nothing is hidden from its heat.

—PSALM 19:1–6

Each soul has its secret place, where none
may enter in save it and God.

—JOHN OXENHAM

12

HE STILL SPEAKS

Terry Toler

HE STILL SPEAKS
By Terry Toler

Amidst a hustling clamoring world
Sometimes it's hard to hear,
The voice of God speaking to my soul;
But in my quiet time alone,
When I approach His holy throne,
His tender words fall gently on my ears.

Chorus

He still speaks, I know His voice,
Sweeter sounds never heard by mortal ear;
And to think that God by His own choice
Would speak to me it makes me rejoice,
He still speaks, I know His voice.

There are so many who still doubt
That God still speaks today,
They laugh and mock
When we say we've heard from God;
But the still small voice of God is heard
Above the doubters of this world,
His timeless word rings out with hope today.

Chorus

> He still speaks, I know His voice,
> Sweeter sounds never heard by mortal ear;
> And to think that God by His own choice
> Would speak to me it makes me rejoice,
> He still speaks, I know His voice.[22]

Songs of Contemplation

I wrote my fist gospel song when I was about fifteen years of age. I still remember the convicting strains of the opening lines: "Have you failed in your prayer life, cut devotions quite short?" The rest of the lines read:

> Is your heart filled with selfish pride, always wanting more?
> Is your life filled with conflict, defeat is everywhere?
> Get closer to God in prayer.

My guess is that I lost a lot of listeners with the opening line. It surely didn't resonate with any publishers. As I look back on my modest song-writing career, "Closer to God in Prayer," which was never published, was actually a prelude to a series of what I call contemplative life songs. "He Still Speaks" falls in that lineage of songs. I'm often asked about how the song was written, if there was some event that inspired it. Honestly, I really do not remember much about the actual writing of the song. I have always believed in the message of the song, and the feedback from listeners is consistent; they resonate with the proposition that God speaks and we can know His voice. The song has had a life of its own, having been recorded by scores of artists—and it's even found its way to YouTube.

Hearing His Voice

God speaking. Man hearing. Man and God communicating—through prayer. To some this seems mysterious and to others, whacky.

A television evangelist says, "God told me. . . ."

A psycho killer says, "God instructed me to. . . ."

A gospel songwriter introduces a composition by saying, "God gave me this song."

How do we make any sense of all this?

Stan, Terry, Mark

Here's what I believe: hearing God's voice is something we all have a deep, innate desire to do. Moreover, I believe that God wants us to hear from Him just as desperately as we want to hear from Him. Psalm 19 has helped my thinking and understanding about what I like to call divine conversations. The focus of the first six verses is on what we see when we look up: the heavens, the skies. Various English translations use the word *firmament*, which refers to the arched dome of the expansive sky that seems to sit on the circle of the earth.

What seems clear to me in this ancient text is that God speaks through everything He has made, and He means for you to hear what He has to say. One of the characteristics of God is His redemptive nature that never wastes anything. He has purpose in all things, yet that purpose may not always be immediately clear. So He never speaks in vain; He intends for what He has to say to minister to you—to meet some need that you have.

Sometimes it may seem like the "heavens are brass" and God is silent; but in reality that is not the case. He is speaking to and through all He has made in this incredible world. And there is constancy to his pattern of speech; it's all day and all night, every day and every night, everywhere in the world.

As a rank amateur when it comes to God talk, I don't pretend to know all the ways that God speaks. I have learned on my faith journey that through prayer, His word and through the Holy Spirit, God is faithful to speak.

THROUGH JESUS CHRIST

Anytime we are confused about what we should do, it's always a good idea to look to Christ our example. Prayer was a constant in His life and was at the heart of all He did. Remember the Jordan River experience with Jesus and John the Baptizer. After Jesus is baptized, something amazing happens: "As soon as Jesus was baptized, he went up out of the water. At that moment heaven was opened, and he saw the Spirit of God descending like a dove and lighting on him. And a voice from heaven said, 'This is my Son, whom I love; with him I am well pleased'" (Matthew 3:16–17). The Father's pleasure in Jesus was not because of what He had done, but because of who He was in relationship to the Father. At that time, Jesus had not performed great miracles, preached the Sermon on the Mount, or called disciples. Jesus was obedient, and that obedience was the result of the relationship the fully God and fully human Jesus had with the Father through prayer. He speaks through prayer.

THROUGH HIS WORD

He also speaks through His word. While I do not worship the Bible, it is God's revelation—His faithful word to all who will hear. The Bible itself declares, "In the beginning was the Word, and the Word was with God, and the Word was God. He was with God in the beginning. Through him all things were made; without him nothing was made that has been made. In him was life, and that life was the light of men" (John 1:1–4). Second

Timothy 3:16 says, "All Scripture is God-breathed and is useful for teaching, rebuking, correcting and training in righteousness."

When the Toler boys were growing up our mother taught us a Bible drill. It went like this, "This book will keep you from sin—or sin will keep you from this book." Then she would have us quote Psalm 119:105: "Thy word is a lamp unto my feet and a light unto my path" (KJV). Early on, our lives we were taught to seek God's word for daily living. So I do believe that God speaks through the Holy Scriptures. I especially find clarity in hearing the voice of God as I study and know the teachings of Jesus and grow in my relationship to Christ. He speaks through the very life of Christ.

THROUGH THE HOLY SPIRIT

Thankfully, in God's divine plan a provision was made for us to continue to hear from the heart of God through the power and presence of the Holy Spirit. Shortly before He was put to death, Jesus spent time with His disciples to reassure them that after He was gone they would not be abandoned as orphans. "And I will ask the Father, and he will give you another Counselor to be with you forever—the Spirit of truth. The world cannot accept him, because it neither sees him nor knows him. But you know him, for he lives with you and will be in you" (John 16:16–17).

THROUGH CREATION

God has and continues to speak to us through prayer, Scripture, and the life of Christ and through the Holy Spirit. I would like to offer one more way God speaks. In Psalm 19, the psalmist describes how God is proclaiming messages through the skies, through what He has made. Those messages reach to the minds and hearts of men and women without the medium of ordinary words or speech.

Have you ever watched a sunrise or sunset and felt tears form in the corners of your eyes, as you behold the magnificent of God's creation? Have you ever stood in holy silence and listened to glaciers as they fall into icy seas? Have you ever heard the voice of God through the rushing torrents at Niagara? Or have you held a newborn baby in your arms? Is there any doubt in your mind that there was a master designer who carefully hand stitched that one-of-a-kind, completely original full image bearer of God?

Even the prolific psalmist struggles to say it. Notice the paradox between these statements: "Day after day they pour forth speech; night after night they display knowledge. There is no speech or language where their voice is not heard." Biblical scholars agree that the same Hebrew word for *speech* is used in both statements. In other words, God means for there to be a connection, communication from His very heart to the heart of mankind. What is often overlooked is that the medium of communication—the means by which this message is carried from His heart to our hearts. In this case, it is neither written nor spoken words; yet it is clear that God is speaking. The heavens declare the glory of God. God is using light, color, shapes, movement and more to reveal a message to all.

One line of the psalm states: "There is no speech or language where their voice is not heard." The next line declares: "Their voice goes out into all the earth, their words to the ends of the world."

Soundless sounds.

Wordless words.

Speechless speech.

Voiceless voices.

The truth is clear: communication is streaming forth from God to us from and through the sky. He is making a declaration in the air. He is skywriting in such a way that everyone who will stop and listen must hear and know that it is God who is speaking.

Who knows what inspired the psalmist? Maybe it was a sunrise so beautiful that as he tried to take it in the Spirit of God quickened his mind and heart to write this powerful text. To help him communicate what the glory of God is really like, He says: "Which is like a bridegroom coming forth from his pavilion, like a champion rejoicing to run his course."

Listening Carefully

Perhaps for you the glory of God seems muted; you haven't experienced it in deep personal ways for some time. May I kindly ask some questions? Not questions that will leave you condemned, but questions that will cause deeper personal reflection:

What are you listening for?
Is there anticipation in your heart that God will speak?
Can you release your faith in greater ways to allow God to speak
in ways you've never known before?

When "He Still Speaks" was written I sent it to a major publisher for consideration. I anxiously awaited a response, and in time a rejection letter came in the mail. It was one of those thanks-but-no-thanks letters. In the providence of God, I received in that very same mail delivery a letter from Gene and Rosemary Lawhun. They were college classmates of mine who were missionaries appointed to Papua New Guinea. In the letter they related that good friends at the church where I was serving had sent them a tape recording of a recent service, which included an early performance of "He Still Speaks."

They described how difficult and sometimes frightening their work was in that remote part of the world. At times discouragement would nearly overtake them. Apparently the cassette with "He Still Speaks" arrived when they were going through a very dark time. The letter told that sometimes, even during the night, they would turn on the tape and play the song again and again. How ironic that a letter of rejection from a major publisher and a letter of reception from faithful missionaries would arrive on the same day.

God was speaking to them through the music and was speaking to me through their faithful lives. He still speaks.

NOTES

1. "Starting Now," Terry Toler & Michael Sykes. Terry Toler Publishing / ASCAP - Mal 'N Al Music / ASCAP. All rights reserved. Used by permission.

2. "He Touched Me," William J. Gaither / Gaither Music Company / ASCAP. All rights controlled by Gaither Copyright Management. Used by permission.

3. Kim Jones, "Bill Gaither Interview," About.com, December 6, 2004, http://christianmusic.about.com/od/interviewsal/a/aabgaither1104.htm (accessed December 28, 2007).

4. "You Can Depend on Jesus," Terry Toler and Rusty Goodman. Terry Toler Publishing / ASCAP - Playin' Tag Music / ASCAP. All rights reserved. Used by permission.

5. "Just Think About," Terry Toler. Terry Toler Publishing / ASCAP. All rights controlled by Integrated Copyright Group. Used by permission.

6. "Remind me, Dear Lord," Dottie Rambo, Bridge Building Music/ASCAP. All rights reserved. Used by permission.

7. "Sweet Communion," Terry Toler. Terry Toler Publishing / ASCAP. All rights controlled by Integrated Copyright Group. Used by permission.

8. Paul J. J. Payak, "The Number of Words in the English Language," The Global Language Monitor, http://www.languagemonitor.com/wst_page7.html (accessed December 28, 2007).

9. Stan Toler and Jerry Brecheisen, Lead to Succeed: New Testament Principles for Visionary Leadership, (Kansas City, Mo.: Beacon Hill Press of Kansas City, 2003).

10. "Child of the King," Cindy Walker, Oree Music/BMI. All rights reserved. Used by permission.

11. "Only Child," Terry Toler & Vic Clay. Universal / ASCAP. All rights reserved. Used by permission.

12. William Barclay, The Letters of John and Jude (Philadelphia: The Westminster Press, 1960), 73.

13. Ibid.

14. "Roll On Church," Public Domain.

15. "I Believe," Jimmy Fortune. Jimmy Fortune Music / BMI. All rights reserved. Used by permission.

16. "Child of the King", Words by Harriet Buell and music by John B. Sumner. Public Domain.

17. "The Shadow of the Steeple," Terry Toler & Rusty Goodman. Universal / ASCAP - Word Music Group / ASCAP. All rights reserved. Used by permission.

18. "The Prodigal Son," Terry Toler. Universal / ASCAP. All rights reserved. Used by permission.

19. "Coming Home," Words and music by William Kirkpatrick. Public Domain

20. "What a Lovely Name," Charles B. Wycuff / Lovely Name Music / ASCAP. All rights controlled by Gaither Copyright Management. Used by permission.

21. "The Happy Goodman Family," Wikipedia: The Free Encyclopedia, http://en.wikipedia.org/wiki/The_Happy_Goodman_Family (accessed December 28, 2007).

22. "He Still Speaks," Terry Toler. Terry Toler Publishing / ASCAP. All rights controlled by Integrated Copyright Group. Used by permission.